The Civil Rights Society

The Civil Rights Society

The Social
Construction
of Victims

**Kristin
Bumiller**

The Johns Hopkins University Press
Baltimore / London

The Johns Hopkins University Press
701 West 40th Street
Baltimore, Maryland 21211
The Johns Hopkins Press Ltd., London

The paper used in this publication meets the minimum requirements of
American National Standard for Information Sciences—Permanence of Paper for Printed Library Materials, ANSI Z39.48–1984. ∞

Library of Congress Cataloging-in-Publication Data

Bumiller, Kristin, 1957–
    The civil rights society.

    Bibliography: p.
    Includes index.
    1. Civil rights—United States. I. Title.
JC599.U5B837 1988   323.4'0973   87-45485
ISBN 0-8018-3544-5 (alk. paper)

For my grandmother, Amo

Contents

Acknowledgments   *ix*

Chapter 1 / The Model of Legal Protection   *1*
   The Civil Rights Consciousness   *4*
   Legal Protection   6
   The Logic of the Law   *9*
   Legitimating Race Policies through Doctrine   *11*
   Individual and Group Rights   *13*
   Private Lives and Public Roles   *15*
   The Critique of Legalism   *19*

Chapter 2 / Law and Ideology   *23*
   Skepticism about Rules   *23*
   The Gap between Legal Ideals and Practice   *25*
   Responses to Discrimination   *26*
   The Study of Legal Consciousness   *30*
   Legal Power   *32*
   Strategies of Method   *33*
   Conclusion   *38*

Chapter 3 / The Historical Roots of Antidiscrimination Ideology   *40*
   Transformation of Ideologies   *40*
   The Birth of Antidiscrimination Law, 1860–1900   *41*
   Civil Rights as a Social Movement, 1950–1972   *46*
   The Historical Construction of Victims   *49*
   The Proliferation of the Civil Rights Strategy   *51*

Chapter 4 / The Ideology of the Victim   *52*
   Carmen   *52*
   Helen   *53*
   Delma   *55*
   Laura   *56*
   The Legal Forum and Victims   *58*
   Identities in the Law   *60*
   Masks of the Victim   *62*
   The Doctrine of Antidiscrimination Law   *64*
   History and Stigma   *66*
   Victims and Power Relations   *69*
   The Manner of Victims   *70*

Chapter 5 / The Ethic of Survival   78
  The Creation of Illegitimate Bonds   78
  Assimilation and Exclusion   84
  An Ethic of Survival   88
  The Politicization of Private Honor   95

Chapter 6 / Legality Enters Life   98
  The Victim's View of the Law   99
  Images of Legality   106

Chapter 7 / Conclusion: Voices Excluded from the Law   109
  Psychology, Politics, and Social Change   112
  Reconstructing the Civil Rights Society   113
  Victims without a Cause   116

Appendix A / List of Interviewees   119

Appendix B / Interview Schedule   121

Notes   125

Bibliography   147

Index   157

Acknowledgments

In this book, I present an alternative vision of the civil rights society that draws upon the strength and courage of those who experience injustice as a part of everyday life. My primary debt is to those people who talked with me about their encounters with discrimination and entrusted me with the responsibility of making some sense out of both their misfortunes and their achievements. Although some will not find the perspective presented here convincing, I have found that friends, colleagues, and students experience similar frustrations and reactions toward the ideology of legal protection, and I hope these efforts provide some understanding of why we are frequently unable to respond adequately to racism or sexism.

I have been fortunate in having benefited from the concern and interest of several persons throughout the completion of this project. I have respected and admired Murray Edelman as a scholar and teacher; I am grateful for his sympathetic readings, which have encouraged me to improve my work without losing compassion for the people whose social position makes them the frequent target of injustice. David Trubek has been helpful every step of the way; I hope he realizes how much his support is appreciated. And Boaventura de Sousa Santos greatly influenced my interpretations and has shown me how friendship and scholarship come together.

The project grew out of questions raised by the Civil Litigation Research Project, supported by the Department of Justice, at the University of Wisconsin-Madison. The interviewees were selected from the surveys conducted by the project. During the early stages of the writing I was supported by a Knapp Graduate Fellowship at the University of Wisconsin-Madison. The Department of Political Science at the Johns Hopkins University has provided a supportive environment for research and writing, and the leave time to complete the manuscript as a Liberal Arts Fellow in Law and Political Science at Harvard Law School. I also had the opportunity to present the work in forums that allowed for feedback and the exchange of ideas, including the Symposium on the Legal History of the Family at the University of Wisconsin-Madison and the conference on Foucault: The History of the Present at the University of California, Berkeley. Portions of this book are published in *Signs: Journal of Women and Culture in Society* under the title "Victims in the Shadow of the Law: A Critique of the Model of Legal

Protection." I would like to thank *Signs* for their editorial assistance, particularly Mary Wyer for her excellent suggestions. In addition, I would like to thank Pietro Belluschi, who enabled me to present on the jacket a symbolic representation of the masks of victimhood by graciously granting permission to reproduce his Jacob Lawrence painting, "*Harlem Series*, no. 2: Most of the people are very poor. Rent is high. Food is high." I also acknowledge the assistance of Ellen Harkins Wheat, the author of a recent book on Jacob Lawrence's art, in locating the jacket artwork.

I also appreciate the efforts of colleagues and friends who have read the manuscript, in whole or in part, at various stages of its completion, including Malcolm Feeley, Martha Fineman, Robert Gordon, Joel Grossman, Norma Kriger, Bert Kritzer, Austin Sarat, Susan Silbey, Jonathan Simon, and Laura Woliver. At the final stages of writing Carol Ehrlich, John Esser, and Daniel Eaton provided helpful assistance. My colleagues at Johns Hopkins have also offered their encouragement; expressly I would like to acknowledge my appreciation to Liliane Weissberg for her friendship and J. Woodford Howard, Jr., for sharing his enthusiasm for the study of law and society. And finally, I am thankful to Larry Rosenthal, whose kindness and optimism have sustained me throughout the writing of this book.

The Civil Rights Society

One / The Model of Legal Protection

The conventional wisdom attributes the failures of antidiscrimination policies during the last two decades to inadequate resources, entrenched cultural biases, and the inevitably slow progress in achieving real economic and social gains. Yet beyond problems of implementation, the inadequacies of antidiscrimination law are inherent within the strategies of equal protection that are advanced by legislation and doctrine. The role of law in promoting social change is problematic when evaluated from the perspective of individuals engaged in conflicts arising from the experience of sexual, racial, and age discrimination. The results of such an approach challenge the conventional faith in the law's ability to eradicate social prejudice and suggest that protective legislation may, in fact, perpetuate patterns of behavior that maintain discriminatory practices.

The twentieth anniversary of the 1964 Civil Rights Act marked the end of an era of uncertain progress. Even though it is difficult to assess complex processes of social and political change, there are many reasons to believe that despite the dramatic victories of the sixties, the civil rights movement did not fulfill its promises. The economic indicators (e.g., levels of unemployment and income) for blacks, women, and other minorities indicate substantial gaps and insubstantial gains relative to the standard of living of the majority.[1] By the 1970s, efforts to eradicate discrimination were confronting strong opposition. Granted, many forms of social segregation have lessened, and this can be seen as both indicator and cause of moderating racial tensions. Many forms of segregation in schools and housing are now illegal, and women and blacks have taken advantage of easier access to professional and other high-paying jobs. This progress, however, coincides with a new realism among groups who experience discrimination—a sense of how little things have changed, even though overt prejudice is less prevalent. Most assessments of the civil rights era show modest progress at best. And there are signs of a growing resentment toward minorities and the possibility that a tide of political conservatism in the 1980s will reverse many of the gains that have been made.

While it is important to be sensitive to those whose courage and extraordinary efforts have contributed to the positive changes that have taken place, we need to explain the failure of civil rights strategies and account for their limited success in initiating long-term activism.

This reassessment arises from an effort to understand the victims' views of the law. The voices of the excluded classes of blacks and women have been quieted in academic work influenced by doctrinal analysis and the dispute-processing paradigm. For that reason, I have chosen to focus on the struggles of women and men, and in particular women of color, because these struggles bear more relevance to the implementation of antidiscrimination policies than the abstract world of legal enactments. The image of the victim that will emerge here is a product of contemporary conditions of sexual and racial oppression: many respond in an ineffectual and defensive manner to a complex network of victimization, and only a few (who are exceptionally prepared for struggle) stage dramatic battles against discrimination. In most accounts of victims in contemporary culture, those who surmount hardships are viewed as champions of social justice and those who are resigned to their disadvantage are treated as the undeserving poor. The perception of the social problem is distorted by both the story of the successful victim and the reinforcement of negative stereotypes. I challenge these mythologies by making known typical situations in which people perceive injustice but are powerless to resist. Much of what has been written about civil rights policies is based on the exceptional cases that reach appellate courts, rather than on cases where individuals have experienced discrimination and have not fought it.

I shall link the substantive insights gained from interviewing victimized individuals with a theoretical and historical analysis of the role of antidiscrimination ideology in structuring social consciousness. In doing so I draw eclectically from theoretical writings by Michel Foucault, Hannah Arendt, Alexis de Tocqueville, Max Weber, and others who comment on the sociology of rights in a democratic society. In particular, Foucault's conceptualization of power and ideology influences my interpretation of sociological interactions and legal discourse.

My central point is that antidiscrimination ideology may serve to reinforce the victimization of women and racial minorities. Instead of providing a tool to lessen inequality, legal mechanisms, which create the legal identity of the discrimination victim, maintain divisions between the powerful and the powerless by means that are obscured by the ideology of equal protection. My approach differs from the conventional view of antidiscrimination policies, which I call "legal protection." Those who accept the reasoning of the legal protection model believe the law to be a powerful and effective instrument because it provides victims with a tool by which they can force perpetrators of unlawful conduct to comply with socially established norms. The model of legal protection assumes that those who have suffered harms will recognize their injuries and invoke the protective measures of law. Since most antidiscrimination laws rely primarily on the victims to identify violations, report them to public authorities, and participate in enforcement proceedings, these laws tacitly assume that such behavior is reasonably unproblematic and that those in the protected class can and will accept those burdens. The model of legal protection is, as I shall later discuss in more detail, a product of the transition from the law of slavery to the post–Civil War legal system; its fundamental premise is that the law can ultimately eliminate economic and social inequality. Thus, during the Reconstruction era many race issues became legal problems that were addressed through a narrow range of strategies that then reemerged during the activism of the civil rights movement and continue to influence contemporary social consciousness.

The failure of legal action is rooted in a social system that maintains inequalities through interpersonal relations. My interviews with victims of discrimination reveal how the social psychology of the victim influences the course of conflicts arising from incidents of discrimination. I offer a critical analysis that views social victimhood as a product of dialectical exchanges between victims and oppressors. The interviews indicate that individuals acquiesce in discrimination struggles by accepting the "invisible bonds of the victim": exclusion, sacrifice, and distortion. These three concepts are derived from a survey of literature on victims including women, concentration camp prisoners, criminals, and witches, and they serve as an analytical device to describe the manner in which the social psychology of victimhood influences and helps maintain asymmetrical power relations.

Victims of discrimination often portray the perpetrators of discrimination as tyrants, for example. The interviews reveal that the bonds of the tyrant image are powerful because they allow the subjects to regard their superiors as immature and arrogant yet justify their own impotence. The image of the tyrant transforms the exchange between perpetrator and victim into a situation in which the perpetrator controls and the victim transgresses. Through detailed examination of responses to discrimination, it becomes clear that these struggles often end in defeat for the victim because the bonds of victimhood inhibit challenges against the perpetrators. The victims internalize the power struggle by submitting to the perpetrator's ruthlessness and to their own anger and confusion. Contrary to the assumption that antidiscrimination law benefits the victim against the more powerful opponent, the bonds of victimhood are reinforced rather than broken by the intervention of legal discourse.

Another example of the social psychology of victimhood is the influence of each individual's ethic of survival on her or his response to discrimination. The ethic of survival defines how individuals view their own struggles and needs. Comparative accounts of individuals' encounters with discriminatory practices, their subsequent choices of action, and the rationalizations for their behavior indicate variation in the degrees to which their self-definition of survival constrains their options. These accounts reveal that (1) victims' responsibility to protect themselves from discriminatory wrongs is subverted by primary responsibilities to other roles, particularly employee, provider for a family, and passive citizen; and that (2) idealized notions of equality or fair treatment may be very costly, given the limited financial, emotional, and social resources that most people have. Therefore, they adopt a stoic stance because their only perceived choice is to endure injustice.

My study goes beyond a sociological account of victimization, because it is ultimately directed toward understanding the role of legal ideology in structuring social conflicts. Part of the inquiry draws upon doctrinal history: reading and interpreting the message about the extent and nature of victims' rights extended by a series of Supreme Court cases in the areas of voting rights, unfair housing and employment practices, and school desegregation. My analysis is, as stated earlier, based on responses from intensive interviews that focus on the victim's view of the law. The victim's perspective directly challenges the assumptions of the model of legal protection. From the victim's point of view there are strong barriers to perceiving their problem as discrimination (that is defensible in court) and establishing a claim as legitimate. People view the law as both protective and destructive, fearing that if they seek a legal resolution they will not gain power but lose control over a hostile situation. They resolve the ambiguity by rejecting the relevance of law to their lives.

The Civil Rights Consciousness

The civil rights movement's antidiscrimination strategy of social change has fundamentally transformed public consciousness. The movement furthered the belief in law that originated during the Reconstruction era: the faith in the power of the law ultimately to change discriminatory attitudes and behavior. The end of societal prejudice was to be brought about by securing egalitarian principles in the law that would establish, in Morroe Berger's words, that the "defenders of the law [were] the defenders of equality." He describes the civil rights effort as a struggle to demonstrate that the idea of equality was not only "a source of genuine superiority in moral position, [but] a source of superiority in political and legal position as well."[2]

The equal treatment of racial minorities in American society has been and continues to be perceived as a "liberal dilemma." The classic

formulation of this paradox is found in Gunnar Myrdal's introduction
to *An American Dilemma* (1944), in which the "race problem" is
described as an embarrassing condition in a prosperous and free nation.
The moral integrity of the society is called into question because
"Negro rights and welfare" pose a contradictory reality in the face of the
optimism of the American creed.[3] Thus, the contradiction between
ideals and practice creates a "social problem" that allows the nation
and, to varying degrees, individuals to rationalize the existence of the
"Negro situation."[4]

Myrdal's perspective was similar to that of other post–World War II
social scientists who were deeply alarmed by the potential for ever-
increasing intolerance in mass society and who advocated the moral
reeducation of the democratic citizen. The hope was that "scientific
truth seeking and education" would slowly modify beliefs that perpetuate racial discrimination.[5] The problem for the liberal, therefore, was a
"white man's problem." Thus, reform was to be achieved through moral
education, or more coercive means of enforcement, directed at the
white majority who exercise the power to change the "Negro's place" in
society. If black Americans had a strategy of their own, it was to identify their cause with the "broader issues in American politics and social
life and with moral principles held dear by the white Americans."[6] The
liberal solution, as originally conceived, was aimed at the moral conver-
sion of the perpetrators and did not foresee the consequences of the
civil rights mentality for its beneficiaries.

Myrdal's characterization of America's dilemma to a greater or lesser
extent orients most liberal commentaries on the "race problem."
Because Myrdal defines race as a moral question, it follows that adjudication is better suited for the resolution of these issues than is political
bargaining. But the liberal dilemma, as it has reemerged in constitutional litigation, is the problem of justifying the courts' special role in
promoting the interests of disadvantaged groups with majoritarian
rule. The liberal justification for legal action depends on the courts'
ability to translate their moral rationale for "special treatment" into
policies that would appear consistent with pluralist politics.

A society transformed by the civil rights consciousness, therefore, is
testing the moral authority of the law. The civil rights consciousness is
a response to the American dilemma—a response that has been created
by the powerful in search of moral exoneration, and its message, although directed at reforming those who perpetuate discrimination,
structures the options for protest for members of the protected class.
The belief in "rights" may extend far beyond their actualization in
statute, case law, and legislation, and their realization in concrete social
situations. Those who hold convictions about the power of the law

may be disadvantaged by their unrealistic expectations. Thus, I shall examine the creation of the antidiscrimination legal consciousness and the consequences of the faith in rights that grew out of the civil rights movement.

Since most accounts of the civil rights movement emphasize the organized protests within the black community beginning in the 1950s, they see the movement solely as an expression of deep moral sentiments and as a symbol of the masses rising up against racial injustice. While periods of persistent activism against racial and sexual inequality have stimulated changes that have opened up possibilities in many people's lives, there is another, more passive side of the civil rights consciousness. The roots of this acquiescence are found within the particular historical circumstances that led to the creation of American race law and the legalistic culture that fostered rights-focused social movements.

Legal Protection

Antidiscrimination doctrine is based upon a model of legal protection. This strategy derives from the Fourteenth Amendment's equal protection clause: "No state shall...deny to any person within its jurisdiction the equal protection of the laws." The historical intent of the clause was to prevent the reenactment of slavery through state legislation. In the original strategy, the equal protection clause initiated a contest between federal and state authority, in which federal authority embodied the ideal of freedom and equality for the newly emancipated slaves.[7] This century has brought the expansion of the equal protection principle through Court interpretations that broaden "state action" and apply the principle to new social groupings. A social problem is recognizable as "discrimination" when it fits the logic of historically evolved antidiscrimination principles.

One fundamental premise of antidiscrimination policies is the limited scope of governmental authority. The "state action" contests, which dominated the early litigation of the civil rights era, forced the courts into a position that accentuated their powerlessness to enforce race-neutral policies in the private sector.[8] To the extent that antidiscrimination policies arbitrate intergovernmental contests of authority, legally relevant discriminatory behavior is limited to cases in which identifiable actions, policies, or rules of the perpetrator harm the victim; the victim claims that local, state, or federal governmental policy allows for discrimination or in other ways benefits the perpetrator; and the victim requests the court to intervene on her or his behalf to challenge the perpetrator's policy. Consider, for example, *Moose Lodge v.*

Irvis,[9] in which the defendant challenged a restriction on black membership by a private club on the ground that the state sanctioned discriminatory practices through granting the club a state liquor license. The Court found the argument insufficient to establish a state interest and ruled in favor of the private club. Through a doctrine of self-limitation, the Court affirmed boundaries between private and public action by narrowly defining the range of governmental activity. The boundaries between public and private in *Moose Lodge* may appear arbitrary, given the pervasiveness of institutionalized forms of racism, but the Court's ability to justify these boundaries reinforces a deeply rooted logic of social change. The strategy of legal protection has evolved so as to be consistent with the role of limited government. When the courts act to strike down race-conscious laws and regulations, they often limit rather than increase governmental intervention in the social and private domain.[10]

The strategy of legal protection is also reflected in the theory and application of the 1964 Civil Rights Act and subsequent civil rights legislation. Similar to state action cases, the contested issue in litigation that arises under these statutes is the boundaries on governmental responsibility to rectify past harms. The definition of discriminatory activity has evolved over the more than twenty-year history of these provisions. The limitations on governmental responsibility are not immediately obvious from the written statute; for example, the employment provisions for Title VII define discriminatory activity broadly in the areas of hiring, discharging, compensation, and other terms, conditions, and privileges of employment such as "to limit, segregate, or classify. . .in any way that would deprive or tend to deprive any individual of employment opportunities or otherwise adversely affect his status."[11]

Despite the seemingly broad scope of the legislation, the courts' interpretation that the burden of proof rests with the complainant severely limits the application of the statutes. The burden of proof can, however, be shifted to the defendant by establishing a prima facie case of discrimination. A prima facie case is made when the plaintiff shows "(i) that [she or] he belongs to a racial minority; (ii) that [she or] he applied and was qualified for a job for which the employer was seeking applicants; (iii) that, despite [her or] his qualifications, [she or] he was rejected; and (iv) that, after [her or] his rejection, the position remained open and the employer continued to seek applicants from persons of complainant's qualifications."[12] Efforts to meet the burden of proof have led plaintiffs to two different ways of demonstrating discriminatory employment practices.

First, relying upon *Griggs v. Duke Power Company*, which promulgated the "adverse impact" doctrine, tests and measuring devices used to screen prospective employees must relate to job performance.[13] At issue, in this case and subsequent rulings, was the validity and appropriateness of standardized tests, employment guidelines (e.g., height and weight), and requirements for training and education that potentially had "disparate impact" on minority groups. Another method of establishing a prima facie case has relied upon statistical data, which is gathered to document, in the company whose policies are under question, the underrepresentation of minorities in relation to the hiring pool.[14] Under some circumstances, discriminatory treatment must be substantiated not only by evidence of disparate impact on minority groups, but by the plaintiff's proof of discriminatory intent.

This complex doctrine provides for exceptions in order not to put unfair burdens upon the employer. The courts have maintained that parties must receive proper notice and that "claims must be timely."[15] The claim must also pass the "business necessity test,"[16] which means that employers are sometimes justified in continuing an employment practice, regardless of its differential racial impact, if the practice is "necessary to safe and efficient operation." In addition, an exception to Title VII is granted if sex is a "bona fide occupational qualification reasonably necessary to the normal operation" of the business. This exception has been used to bar women from dangerous occupations such as prison guard and to justify policies against hiring women with preschool-age children.

Neither can antidiscrimination regulations interfere with poor treatment of employees when it is not limited to persons of one race or sex. In *Bradford v. Sloan Paper Co.*,[17] the federal district court ruled that employers may be abusive to minority employees (including threat of physical violence) as long as they are "equally offensive to both races." And finally, the employer and white employees cannot bear the burden of past discrimination. For example, the Court has found that some types of affirmative action policies violate the vested rights of the white employees implied by the employment contract.[18]

These are a few examples of the limitations placed on plaintiffs engaged in employment discrimination suits.[19] Activists have called for expanding the scope of protection to cover a wider range of harms and to reflect more adequately the difficulties of substantiating a case.[20] The more expansive interpretations, however, would not modify the basic premises of the model of legal protection.

The Logic of the Law

Antidiscrimination policies follow a strategy of incremental reform. Rhetorically this view is often presented in judicial decisions through contrasting the soon-to-be-achieved egalitarian future with sweeping historical references to the extreme conditions of slavery and economic servitude.[21] The slow progress is justified by the assumption that the cycle of prejudice is defeated by gradual reform and attitudinal change, which in turn promotes a democratic citizenry receptive to the advancement of disadvantaged groups. Furthermore, the role of the courts in moving society toward racial equality is limited by the competing values of local autonomy, administrative efficiency, and social justice for the majority. Some legal advocates have faith that its internal logic drives the equal protection doctrine to broader conceptions of gender and race discrimination and removes, step by step, other obstacles to successful claims. Others see the development of antidiscrimination law as inconsistent: *Brown v. Board of Education* began an era of dramatic expansion through the proclamation of abstract rights and then evolved into a period of retraction when the courts focused on practices rather than results.[22] In this view, antidiscrimination policies do not embody absolute standards; instead, the protections guaranteed by law are "evolving" and conform to "present practices."

The application of the law, of course, requires cases.[23] In addition to the difficulties of determining whether the current status of the law recognizes the claim as legitimate, only a particular type of social incident can be translated into a legal claim of discrimination. First, a prototypical case must demonstrate that the individual has suffered from a public harm. Behavior is considered discriminatory in a legal sense when the alleged harmful actions attain public significance. The law is not designed to prevent people from imposing their private preferences or tastes for discrimination, even though prejudicial actions may have serious and detrimental consequences for the victim. Racial insults or segregation that occurs in private social settings does not fall into the range of harms that can be remedied in court. Yet the boundaries between public and private activity are constantly subject to debate, and are modified by new interpretations of the antidiscrimination principle; for example, sexual harassment, once considered a private dispute between men and women in the workplace, has acquired recognition as a form of sex discrimination.[24]

Second, discrimination cases are time-bound and isolated incidents in individuals' lives. A claim of right is a legal entitlement granted to individuals pursuing their interests in a social transaction. Since antidiscrimination laws grant protection to all citizens, rather than to a group or class, the claim must be presented as a violation of an individual interest.[25] In addition, the prototypical case involves incidents that are subject to just compensation. The actions against the perpetrator provided by the law are nonpunitive; therefore, the courts play a limited role unless the victim can be compensated. The theory applied is "wrongs may be justly punished, but only measurable wrongful harms can be justly compensated."[26] The victim who suffers only from emotional harm or prefers to seek other employment or accommodations may not have grounds for a legal claim.

In the model of legal protection, the mobilization of the law is the link between the people and the law.[27] The operation of a responsive legal system, as described by the nineteenth-century German legal instrumentalist Rodolph von Jhering, relies upon citizens' seeing their moral duty to use the law to prevent infringement of their rights and to ensure that law maintains its power.[28] The lamented failure of the responsible citizen, the fear that citizens will abrogate the power of government, is the linchpin in the theory of legal protection—for the victim must cooperate with the state. The assumption is that citizens are delegated a part of the police power of the polity; that victims discover and report violations in a joint effort with the state against the perpetrators. Thus, the principle of antidiscrimination imparts a shared guilt to the victims for their failure to achieve their own protection. The active enforcement of antidiscrimination law also depends on the level of mobilization among the citizenry. Analogous to the economic market, enforcement increases or decreases with the victims' reporting of rule-violating behavior.[29]

The model of legal protection reinforces a view of law and society in which the social and political realm is distinct from, and subordinate to, the legal. This view of the primacy of the legal order creates the illusion that law is a source of power and authority disconnected from other power structures in society.[30] Thus, legality has its origins in the pathology of social relations; conflicts, such as racial discontent, are seen as aberrational incidents that occur when the social structure breaks down, and the introduction of the law maintains order.

Antidiscrimination doctrine sets bounds on the relationship between the state, the citizen, and the law. The deep logic of the law does not reflect the complex social reality of discrimination in society, but rather confines legal resolution to social problems appropriate for litigation. In the contemporary civil rights society, in which law is seen as an effective instrument of social change, appeal to the law is taken for granted as the only possible course for progressive reform. Yet, as the assumptions within legal discourse are made explicit, we shall see that the legal logic is directed to limiting social transformation rather than facilitating it.

Legitimating Race Policies through Doctrine

Despite the quieting of racial unrest since the height of the civil rights movement, racism persists in both obvious and insidious forms. My analysis begins with the assumption that racism and sexism are prevalent, and is sympathetic to those who are impatient with the current rate of progress toward a more egalitarian society. The effects of racial prejudice have not lessened in the last decades. Examples include isolated instances of racially motivated violence, the continuation of segregated housing patterns, the disparities of income and standard of living (including infant mortality rates), and the fear of interracial crime. The political discourse of the civil rights society has lost its moral urgency, however, and has taken on the more rationalized tone of legal decision makers.

The language of civil rights that has been adopted by the American legal elite who comment on Supreme Court decision making is called *process theory*. Process theories have the objective of reconciling antidiscrimination measures that benefit the interests of a minority with the constitutional restrictions on democratic authority. These theories are advanced by progressives, who hope to justify the expansion of efforts to eradicate discrimination, yet are aware of the consequences of the undemocratic nature of these efforts for the legitimacy of the courts.

Process theorists attempt to broaden the scope of antidiscrimination doctrine to combat institutionalized racism and economic disadvantage, but without altering the doctrine's basic design. For example, the move from the unconstitutionality of school segregation to the determination of appropriate remedies drove the Court from a reasoning based on status harm to process theory. In *Brown* the Court relied upon a theory of harm that compelled it to rectify the stigmatizing of small children imposed by the segregation of schools. By the *Green* decision in 1968,[31] the Court was forced to evaluate the underlying motives that led to "racially identified schools" and the integrity of political decision making by local school boards.[32] The Court has also found itself in a quandary over what makes a law racially discriminatory, and has had to develop ground rules that trigger close scrutiny in order to restrict legislation that is not discriminatory on its face but has obvious racial impact. Since the 1960s the Court has been moving toward a theory of group rights, accepting Myrdal's premise in *An American Dilemma* that groups with a history of mistreatment suffer from the effects of hostility, and this in turn reinforces their victimization and prevents them from using the instruments of power to benefit the interests of the group.

Process theories are elaborate defenses of the neutrality of judicial decision making.[33] These theories account for process failure, the breakdown of normal channels of representation, and then show how corrective measures fit into the scheme of democratic government. John Hart Ely's *Democracy and Distrust*, for example, justifies the expansion of the equal protection clause more specifically as a constitutional articulation of the value of participation. He argues that contemporary conditions of racial discrimination are much the same as those Madison saw when he pointed to the danger of factions tyrannizing the interests of minorities. When the Court intervenes to protect the interests of minorities, therefore, it protects the "process" of democratic government by opening up the channels of representation.[34] Since the full benefits of representative government are unattainable for groups hindered by social and economic inequalities, the Court's "representational reinforcing" role compensates for denied access. The appeal of Ely's theory is that it portrays the Court as a defender of the process of democracy when it exercises judicial scrutiny over democratically elected legislatures.[35]

The neutrality of the "representational reinforcing" role becomes questionable, however, as soon as the Court moves beyond the easy cases, such as those concerning voting rights, in which there is a direct connection between hostile governmental policies (i.e., restrictions on registration) and the proper functioning of representative government. In the hard cases of economic and social disadvantage, it is more difficult to employ process theories to justify appropriate levels of judicial "suspicion" of governmental policies. In these cases, the Court's suspicion is not triggered by the formal requirements of access, but by the effect of governmental policies on the minority group's ability to combat hostilities. The principle of neutrality is weakened when the Court is required to make empirical evaluations (i.e., determining whether the law negatively stereotypes minorities or evaluating minorities' abilities to "represent themselves").[36] Process logic, because it legitimizes the evaluation by (chiefly white, male, nonpoor) judges of the conditions of political subjugation and the political relevance of shared group interests, evolves into a theory of representation in which groups neither define nor advocate their own interests.

Ultimately, process theory defends the Court from criticism only in easy cases. The more widespread the disadvantage, the more likely that courts will be put in the position of either transforming the structure of power or justifying the accumulation of hostile legislation.[37] The move toward greater equality is inhibited by judicial self-restraint or external cries about the capacity of the courts to promote social change.[38]

Individual and Group Rights

Process theory is a defense of Court actions that strike down laws or procedures that disproportionately restrict disadvantaged groups. The legitimacy of these actions is called into question because often the Court is unable to establish a direct link between the harm suffered by individuals and a perpetrator committing wrongful acts. Thus, it is argued that the Court has abandoned the notion of individual rights for the protection of *group rights*.

The tension between group and individual rights stems from the theory of individual safeguards in the Constitution and the wording of the Fourteenth Amendment. The historical purpose of the equal protection clause was to protect the interests of a particular group, but its designers deliberately chose a wording of the clause that stated its purpose as the equal protection of "persons" under law. The Court has consistently rejected the idea of "natural" classes (of which blacks would be the prototypical group). Through the conceptual device of "suspect classification" the Court has been able to consider the effects of past discrimination on a group, yet leave the reference to groups malleable so as to keep their decisions consistent with the "ideal of treating people as 'individuals.' "[39] In other words, references to groups are continually scrutinized by the Court to assure that they do not offend the value of individuality.

Those who object to group rights believe there is an inconsistency between the civil rights vision and the American ideal of individualism. While progressive legal reformers call attention to the "condition" of blacks or the "black situation" as the origin and path for solutions for racial inequalities, neoconservatives are alarmed that the focus on the "race problem" has resulted in affirmative action and other policies that benefit blacks as groups rather than as individuals.[40] They find fault in antidiscrimination policies that assume that everyone is guilty and therefore should share in the social costs.[41] These policies are viewed as offensive because statistical parity and minority group consciousness are considered incompatible with an American society based on consensus.

Neoconservatives claim that the American consensus is founded on the belief that there are no group rights. In their vision of American society as a melting pot, no group is required to give up the totality of its group character or ethnic identity to win admission to mainstream American society. The melting pot society protects both majority and minority interests: the majority benefits from the unique contributions of culturally diverse groups, while the minorities are admitted into society with their ethnic identities intact. Nathan Glazer predicts that group rights will produce a perversion of the American ideal of equality, leading to an "Orwellian nightmare" in which some groups will be more equal than others: "Individuals find subtle pressures to make use of their group affiliation not necessarily because of any desire to be associated with a group but because groups become the basis for rights, and those who want to claim certain rights must do so as a member of an affected or protected class."[42]

The problem with neoconservatives' arguments is that they consider group and individual rights as mutually exclusive. They also regard the current design of affirmative action policies as the only imaginable articulation of group rights, rather than a feeble invocation of the idea of group rights. Current policies of group preference assume that the machinery of racism or sexism can be subverted by compensatory practices, thus ignoring the entrenched nature of prejudice and the multiplicity of factors that contribute to racial and ethnic boundaries. Antidiscrimination policies project a meaning of rights that is neither true to its individualist nature nor unambiguous about sustaining group interests. A novel theory of group rights may uphold policies that provide special benefits for groups (e.g., privileges for women associated with childbearing and day care) and may candidly evaluate laws on the basis of whether the practice "aggravates the subordinate position of a specially disadvantaged group."[43] This conception of group rights is based on an ideal of equality that recognizes sameness as well as difference. The full recognition of the rights of social groups, however, may undermine the individualist and incremental logic of equal protection by encouraging intense political competition among the most disadvantaged groups in American society.

The issue of group versus individual rights, as it has been posed in the process theory debate, ignores the multiple identities and mutual responsibilities that mold social relationships.[44] Members of ethnic, racial, and sexual groups have multiple identities based on both individualist and group-oriented roles. They may encounter harms that arise from a cluster of factors that relate to group-based and personal identities. Or their deprivation may result from a combination of group identities, such as the discrimination experienced by single black mothers. A meaningful idea of rights, given the reality of complex social identities, would not be based on a polar opposition between group rights and individual rights but would reflect the forces of disempowerment that reinforce hierarchies in society.

Private Lives and Public Roles

The debate over contemporary civil rights policy converges on the issue of the legitimacy of state intervention in the economy and social life. The degree of state intervention required by antidiscrimination measures is scrutinized and balanced against violations of democratic values, the market economy, and "natural" processes of assimilation of minority groups.

Discrimination and the Market

Free market economists deny the link between discrimination and poverty, claiming that "statistical disparities" reflect the reality of group patterns that may not "arise and persist without discrimination, [but]... if they do, then discrimination takes its place as only one cause among many."[45] They insist that the atmosphere for litigation is too permissive, allowing individuals to stack the deck against their employers by shopping around for statistical breakdowns of minority representation that put the employer in the worst light.[46] Hence, these statistical disparities are acceptable because society has no "moral responsibility" to rectify injustices that reflect a "baseline" of intergroup differences arising from environmental and historical causes.[47]

The neoconservatives bolster their argument by citing the cost of civil rights programs to properly functioning competitive markets and to minority groups. They claim that minority groups have already demonstrated the "potential for success" and were aided only by the doctrine of equal protection, which existed prior to the enactment of affirmative action measures.[48] Consequently, affirmative action exacts too high a cost from white society (which they assume is not guilty of creating situations of disadvantage) and from minorities who are likely to experience retaliation.

These costs to society are measured as deviations from the hypothetical neoclassical model of fair competition (Becker-Arrow model).[49] Those who object to the market disruptions caused by antidiscrimination measures refer to a hypothetical world in which the actors, both victims and perpetrators, make decisions about employment based on economic incentives. In these "transactions," the actors make their choices freely and with full information. Economic models assess the impact of racial or sexual discrimination by accounting for the effects of supply and demand on income differentials. After adjusting for factors such as age, education, marital status, and occupational classification, the significant gaps in white versus black or female wages that remain are due to employers' "taste for discrimination." Therefore, economic discrimination is the result of market imperfections that can be combated through disincentives to employers who would otherwise exercise their biases in hiring decisions. The idealized economic model relies on the assumption that the enforcement of equal opportunity laws would diminish the impact of market imperfections and ultimately close the gap in wage differentials.

The hypothetical economic model reinforces the individualistic logic of legal doctrine. By emphasizing the role of legal authority in changing the incentives of employers, the model ignores the disadvantages created in the marketplace by differences in group background and market-valued characteristics that are likely to persist in conditions of equal economic opportunity.[50] Differences in groups' position in the labor force are produced by motivational factors such as workers' expectation of success in the job market. Even when previously excluded groups enter the labor force, their gains may be offset by increases in the more advantaged groups' occupational position and salary. More intricate processes of discrimination result from the link between social and economic lives. Many women who become heads of households after the breakup of the family or motherhood are unable to break out of a cycle of economic dependency and are ill-prepared to improve their economic status. Women and minorities are segregated into "economic ghettos," that is, occupations with lower training requirements and that permit career interruptions (but that pay lower wages and provide little room for advancement). Or they may take on the role of secondary earners within the family and perhaps be driven in and out of employment with economic trends. These patterns produce the situation in which job segregation encompasses wage discrimination, by forcing women and racial minorities into lower-paying and lower-status jobs.[51]

These subtle forms of discrimination often arise from interactions between employers and workers and the role perceptions held by and imposed on women and racial groups. These factors promote economic discrimination that cannot be compensated for through further corrections of market failures. As with process theory, there is no direct link between the harms experienced and the illegal action or prejudicial treatment by employers. Moreover, these inequalities are unlikely to be removed from the workplace without restructuring the basic design of worker supply and demand to recognize the interests of employees in other than economic terms.

Discrimination and Private Lives

Whereas antidiscrimination doctrine attempts to affirm the boundaries between the state and the economy in order to preserve the integrity of the market, the boundaries between state and society are desired to preserve the well-being of the Republic. Since the structure of civil rights protest pitted the activist against the recalcitrant state official, the common assumption of political discourse is that the more progressive position advocates a strong governmental role in changing prejudicial attitudes and behavior. These assumptions about public roles and private lives are challenged in Hannah Arendt's provocative essay "Reflections on Little Rock." Arendt's framing of these questions deserves extended consideration because it emphasizes the political dimensions of these boundaries.

Arendt's article brought strong opposition from those who believed that her objections to federal intervention in the desegregation of Little Rock's schools were based upon a strain of elitism and flagrant disregard for the plight of blacks in the South. This criticism may underestimate her sympathies for the minority situation, but her concerns were primarily for the "well-being" of the political life of the Republic rather than "the well-being of the Negro population alone."[52] Agreeing with Tocqueville's warnings about the dangers of equality, Arendt suggests that "the more equal people become in every respect, and the more equality permeates the whole texture of society, the more will differences be resented, and the more conspicuous will those become who are visibly and by nature unlike others."[53] She suggests a view of assimilation that reflects her European Jewish heritage, an experience that taught her that political emancipation would not necessarily lead to social equality.[54] Since the visibility of the black minority was permanent, she feared that greater political equality would both increase white resentment and suppress the cultural expression of "blackness."

Arendt's diagnosis of the desegregation problem is based upon her distinction between public and private life.[55] Her interpretation of the proper role of government relies upon her categorizations of political, social, and private spheres. Discrimination is legitimate activity in the social sphere; it allows for free association and group formation. Without social discrimination, mass society would be driven toward conformism. She explains that "discrimination is as indispensable a social right as equality is a political right. The question is not how to abolish discrimination, but how to keep it confined within the social sphere, where it is legitimate, and prevent its trespassing on the political and the personal sphere, where it is destructive."[56] The purpose of federal intervention, therefore, is not to combat the "social custom" of discrimination, but its legal enforcement. The focus of civil rights activity should be violations of the personal sphere in existing law, such as antimiscegenation laws or restrictions on political expression such as bars on voting in the South.

The problem with federal enforcement of school desegregation is that it affects overlapping realms of human life: the political interests of the state in civil rights, the social sphere of freedom of choice, and the private rights of parents to supervise their children's education. Arendt's deepest fears are that the desegregation of schools will produce a situation in which the child is stigmatized by being forced into a social environment where she or he is not wanted. She alludes to a photograph in a magazine reporting the Little Rock incident "showing a Negro girl, accompanied by a white friend of her father, walking away from school, persecuted and followed into bodily proximity by a jeering and grimacing mob of youngsters. The girl, obviously, was asked to be a hero—that is, something neither her absent father, nor the equally absent representatives of the NAACP felt called upon to be."[57] Arendt goes on to ask, "Have we come to the point where it is the children who are being asked to change or improve the world?" Arendt's sympathies lie with the child who is forced to undergo the burdens of harassment and the parent who would refuse to subject her child to this torment.

Ralph Ellison has suggested that Arendt was wrong in her judgment about Little Rock because she misunderstood the basic heroism of the "Negro struggle." Ellison wrote:

> I believe that one of the important clues to the meaning of the Negro experience lies in the idea, the ideal of sacrifice. Hannah Arendt's failure to grasp the importance of this ideal among Southern Negroes caused her to fly way off into left field in her "Reflections on Little Rock" in which she charged Negro parents with exploiting their children during the struggle to integrate the schools. . . . [S]he has absolutely no conception of what goes on in the minds of Negro parents when they send their kids through those lines of hostile people. . . . [The child] is required to master the inner tensions created by his racial situation, and if he gets hurt—then his is one more sacrifice. It is a harsh requirement, but if he fails this basic test, his life will be even harsher.[58]

The disagreement between Ellison and Arendt centers on the importance of the reality of the personal struggle. Ellison points out that the evaluation of personal costs cannot be made outside the context of struggle and sacrifice in individuals' lives. In terms of the hopelessness of black existence in the South during the 1950s, sacrifice was a necessary and required ingredient of confronting and resolving racial tensions. Arendt, in her compelling but ultimately misguided writings, brings to the debate the human dimension of struggle, sacrifice, and survival.

The contemporary struggle against racial discrimination has the appearance of challenging the accepted boundaries between social, economic, and political life. The public policy tug of war stretches the line between high and low levels of governmental intervention, yet never questions the basic integrity of the economic market or the reality of personal lives. The result is a policy debate that depersonalizes the human dimension of the struggle against racism and sexism and that assumes that restructuring society to prevent the reinforcement of hierarchies is impractical or undesirable.

The Critique of Legalism

The design of civil rights programs appears controversial, but media and academic commentaries have in common the belief that legal solutions are desirable and that legal criteria should determine the boundaries of affirmative action measures. There is, however, another voice, which has questioned the role of law. This dissent began within the internal struggles of civil rights protest organizations.

The protest activities during the 1960s and 1970s radicalized many protesters who saw disadvantages in working through the system. Dr. Martin Luther King, Jr., and others who adhered to a strategy of assimilation and integration were confronted by radicals who favored collective action mobilized by the slogan "black power."[59] While King believed that the symbolism of black power would lead to a suicidal confrontation, the slogan's proponents insisted that the civil rights struggle must center on a policy of self-determination.[60] The radicals justified violence to produce results if liberal reform became intolerably slow. As they saw it, civil rights legislation was aimed at pacification and amounted to no more than the continuation of "white Americans still having the power to decide just what rights blacks should have and what rights blacks should not have."[61] The end result of black interest-group activity would be a "united liberal image" that would not "speak to the real needs of the people."[62] The impact of these more radical groups and factions within moderate groups was lessened by their own problems of leadership and by government officials who sabotaged their efforts.[63]

The disillusionment with litigation extended to the disenchanted liberal who saw excessive faith in the "myth of rights," the view that the law corrects the failures of the democratic process. The myth of rights ascribes a privileged role to the courts and furthers the belief that they promote a stable constitutional order. This resulted in the misleading impression that courts are all-powerful, when the record of court activity during the 1960s revealed that courts were most effective at promoting social change when their decisions did not intervene deeply in social and political institutions.[64] In school desegregation cases, for example, the Court was effective at articulating fundamental values, but traveled along an uncertain path in decisions that focused on desegregation plans.[65] Stuart Scheingold argues that the myth of rights may deceive strategists with the assumption that rights are self-enforcing, yet he acknowledges that rights are important agents of mobilization:

> It is thus possible to view the civil rights era as a time of "colloquy" among judges, legislators, and administrators, a colloquy which was fruitful precisely in the measure that segregationist politics had been discredited by judicial initiative. The judges' function was, in other words, to call attention to the enduring principles of American politics—to what I have termed constitutional values—and in this way to demonstrate the dangers inherent in the expedient compromises that are the inevitable consequence of political bargaining.[66]

The disenchanted liberal grants that the courts play a limited role as social policy makers.[67] This perspective informs civil rights activists that their movement should not be dominated by "legalism," because it is an inherently conservative strategy that will lead the movement through a path of frustration. The disenchanted liberal, however, merely redesigns the battle plan to recognize that mobilization must go beyond the courtroom and should proceed without total reliance on a strategy based on "rights."

The disillusionment runs deeper to suspicions that legal strategies are deceptive because they rely on the myth that racial discrimination is a unique form of oppression. According to Derrick Bell, civil rights law has a "fairy tale quality," shrouding contradictions with symbols of hope and redemption.[68] Legal symbols "expunge the dark skin" of law; in the long run they fail, "and blacks find themselves. . .trapped in the darkness of a new and more subtle set of subordinating social shadows."[69] The radical believes that these myths have justified the courts' policy of allowing only small increments of progress rather than promoting redistributive policies. The result is, as Alan D. Freeman says, the "bourgeoisification" of a small group of the minority class who became the visible legitimation of class inequalities.[70]

The radical critique claims that discrimination is maintained and perpetuated by existing legal practices. There are three lines of contention: (1) bias labeled as "discretionary" action has severe "discriminatory" effects;[71] (2) existing law and doctrine that appears neutral on its face discriminates against the poor and minorities;[72] and (3) legal inaction results in the failure of any affirmative effort to rectify wrongs against the victimized class.[73] Each point emphasizes that the eradication of "racism on the surface" does not eliminate the racist consequences of the system's policies.

The critics of rights-focused litigation maintain that the manipulation of doctrine preserves the illusion that law will fulfill its promises. The notable victories for equal opportunity promote a false optimism, either by creating the impression that the problem has been solved or by making a series of inconsistent (or regressive) Court actions appear consistent. Rather than accepting the legacy of Court decisions since *Brown* as evidence of social progress, the radical denounces legal manipulations aimed at avoiding fundamental political and social change. Alan Freeman suggests that the courts have limited the expansion of antidiscrimination policies "by separating violation from remedies."[74] Freeman argues that the early discrimination cases (1954–65) marked an era of "jurisprudence of violations." The courts adhered to the principles suited to "formalistic, positivist jurisprudence" by avoiding substantive purposes and focusing attention on legislative means (i.e., evaluating the overinclusiveness of legislative action) and on application of the "fundamental right" rationale to affirm formal and procedural rights. Freeman demarcates a second time period, lasting until the early 1970s, as the era of contradiction. When forced into the position of prescribing remedies in school desegregation, voting, and employment cases the courts made few decisions (e.g., *Griggs v. Duke Power Company*) that focused concerns on identifying violators and recognizing the discriminatory consequences of apparently neutral practices. The doctrinal approach taken by the Supreme Court since the midseventies, moreover, has led to a halt in the expansion of equal protection doctrine, largely by reliance on the assumption that a society without racial discrimination already exists and that discrepancies are aberrations.

The radical critique is forceful and important to the extent that it characterizes antidiscrimination law as a hegemonic structure of thought that protects a liberal consensus resistant to imposing the costs of past and present racial oppression on the majority. Yet these criticisms are most often expressed by pointing out the internal contradictions in legal doctrine, rather than examining the law in the context of everyday struggles.[75]

The feminist disappointment in legalism has struck a different tone than the radicalization of the struggle against racism. The radical feminist came to realize that the ideology of equality, once translated into divorce legislation, employment law, and family law, was disadvantageous to women who did not live up to preexisting "male standards."[76] Some feminists have advocated a "difference" approach that seeks legal recognition for needs of women that arise out of situations in which the interests of fairness require unlike treatment for women and men (e.g., pregnancy leave). This new version of rights discourse raises the specter of "special protection" for those who are reminded of legislative restrictions on the freedom of women, but for others there is the prospect of legal recognition of the structure of male domination.[77]

The influence of feminist theory and practice on legal criticism has stimulated interest in the effects of law on the experiences of women. This scholarship has found a "different voice": the voice of an excluded class of persons that bears no resemblance to its characterization in legal and psychological theory.[78] For some feminists, this voice reflects the distinctive morality of women, focused on issues of caring and community rather than justice and autonomy, while for others, the voice may be a product of the differences in socialization experiences of an oppressed group. The feminist perspective does not accept the male orientation toward law and legal roles; instead, it advocates "analysis [that]...takes women rather than law" as its starting point.[79]

In this book I explore these strains of skepticism about legal reform by examining how members of the "protected classes" respond to the civil rights consciousness. I take seriously the reservations about rights-focused strategies that have been expressed in the radicals' retrospective evaluations of the civil rights movement. The easy dismantling of civil rights policies, particularly affirmative action efforts, in the 1980s has provided a lesson about the fragility of the earlier victories. Moreover, those most deeply involved in civil rights activities have questioned the "high price that continued reliance on litigation exacts": the inability to move toward "more dynamic attacks on the real causes of our subordinate status."[80] Whether or not rights discourse can be an asset for those engaged in the civil rights struggle remains a vexing question.

Two / Law and Ideology

Skepticism about Rules

The official language of the law is the principal attraction in legal interpretation. Legal doctrine and case law are often the text and documents for public discussion and academic analysis. The authoritative discourse of judges, legislators, and administrators is given preferred meaning, as if these legal messages reflect an inevitable and superior reality. Those who criticize the legal order are often as enamored of the official law as those who espouse it.

Modern legal thinkers have sought to revise legal practices by grounding legal knowledge on external criteria, such as social or moral custom, rather than legal rules. In the United States, these thinkers reacted against classical legal formalism, which rose to its height in the late nineteenth century and facilitated the rapid economic expansion that was taking place.[1]

The critique of legal formalism began with the growth of philosophical pragmatism in American universities and social engineering on the bench and became known as the legal realism movement in law schools (1920–40). The legal realists were reformers who viewed law as a social experiment, a purposeful instrument for engineering a more efficient and just social order. The realists applied their pragmatic vision to moving law beyond the prerequisites of procedure and fairness to a more flexible legal order capable of adapting to the public interest and social change.[2]

The realists created diverse intellectual traditions, but they had in common skepticism toward legal rules and a strong reaction against abstract "conceptualism." The broadening of the study of legal behavior from the "law in the books" to the "law in action" was brought about by the legal realists' recognition of the role of facts in judicial decision making and their interest in the social reality of the lawyer's office, the judge's chambers, and institutional settings where laws were enforced. The realists agreed that rules did not accurately describe social reality, and that in order to move toward a more effective legal system scholars and practitioners had to pay attention to the everyday life of the law.

As Lon Fuller explains in his qualified critique of the movement, rule skepticism was based on two related grounds: "The first lies in a conviction that 'reality' is a thing too complex, tumultuous, and vital to be kept in a straightjacket of rules. . . .The other ground for [this] distrust of rules lies not so much in a belief in the impossibility of the task imposed on rules as in a belief in the *essential impotence of rules themselves*."[3] The first strain of rule skepticism, the law and society tradition, emphasized the compatibility of the reformers' pragmatic legal philosophy with the methodological foundations of the newly emerging social sciences. By their own description, this tradition did not claim to transform law but only to modify the methodology and improve the accuracy by which we describe the legal world. Although the realists had policy-oriented goals, they were influenced by a view of social science that dictated, particularly at the fact-gathering stage, value-neutral inquiry. The realists held on to the belief that there is objective knowledge about law. In fact, they substituted the methodological tenets of social science for the rigors of deductive logic.

There was a more critical strain of realism, one that proposed a different way of thinking about law. An underlying current of the movement was the critique of the language of legal reasoning. Its proponents hoped that empiricism would bring life to legal thought, which had been dominated by artificial abstractions. And these more critical realists did not believe that the rigid conceptions of orthodox legal reasoning made sense in the context of analytical and psychological processes of individuals. The more skeptical realists were influenced by psychology—for example, Jerome Frank attributed the realists' dislike of mechanical jurisprudence to their view of the relationship between the individual and the law, a paternal bondage in "the kingdom of justice." The submission to a father-judge authority figure offered the security found in completeness and finality, yet created a childlike emotional dependence.[4] Implicit in Frank's version of realism was distrust of law as an instrument of authority.

The critique of legal authority implied in the scholarship of Frank and other realists has been, for the most part, dismissed in the study of law and society, even as interest has grown in the law in action. The initial policy interests of the realist have led to the formulation of research problems that are limited to the issues of legal effectiveness, deterrence, and the implementation of legal rules. In the study of civil rights policies, for example, empirical analysis has focused on the problems of enforcement. The effectiveness of legal rules, in practice, is evaluated not by the impact of legal rules on potential litigants, but by the impact of sanctions imposed on the perpetrators. This research often assumes that an effective antidiscrimination policy relies on the compliance, either voluntary or mandatory, of employers, admissions boards, and others who potentially engage in discriminatory practices.

Even when researchers focus their attention on the potential litigants, they often uncritically assume that these individuals act according to the individualistic and rational model implied in the logic of legal protection. Thus, the pragmatic vision of the realists tightly constrains our thinking—in general, about the role of law in social reform, and in particular, about protective legislation such as antidiscrimination policies. These skeptics raised the question, however, that should continue to guide empirical research: How do we create purposeful legal rules that lead law and society closer to its ideals?

The Gap between Legal Ideals and Practice

Research into law and society has evaluated the effectiveness of antidiscrimination policies and has found a substantial gap between the objectives of enforcement and the outcomes of incidents of discrimination. Leon Mayhew's pioneering study, *Law and Equal Opportunity*, examined the Massachusetts Commission against Discrimination (MCAD) in the 1960s. Mayhew found that although the public record of the commission documented a high success rate, this was achieved through statistical manipulation: claims not fully investigated were categorized as "dismissed for lack of probable cause." This created the impression that the greatest difficulty in administering antidiscrimination law was the scarcity of "good complaints." The commission's mentality fostered the belief that the difficulties of enforcement did not rest with the capacity of the law to deal with discrimination claims. The commission justified the systematic exclusion of claims through an uncritical acceptance of the legal criterion that distinguishes a successful discrimination case.[5]

A more recent study of the Massachusetts Commission against Discrimination found that complainants, in general, had unsuccessful experiences.[6] The lower-class complainants were more dissatisfied than upper-class individuals, primarily because they made fewer demands and were less involved in their cases. For the MCAD sample, dealing with the commission was an emotionally charged and negative experience. The defendants felt that they were being put on the defensive—as if the degradation of the commission hearing was a double punishment. The researcher suggested that the actual impact of commission enforcement was not success for a few clients but that "the failures of MCAD would increase or at least perpetuate discrimination by those respondents who suffered little or no penalty."[7] The failure of the commission gave a sense of security to the perpetrators because it indicated that discrimination was so widespread that they could not be singled out for enforcement. More systematic research examining commissions throughout the nation has revealed that commissions have virtually abandoned case-by-case enforcement and have concentrated their efforts on targeted perpetrators with limited success and considerable suspicion of co-optation.[8]

Despite the overwhelming evidence that the enforcement of anti-discrimination policies has been a dismal failure, these researchers have failed to question the power of the law to bring about social change.[9] Often the conclusion of these empirical inquiries has been that the gap between ideal and social practice can be closed by improving policy and its implementation. My examination of the civil rights society observes a similar pattern of failure, but takes this pattern as the starting point for further inquiry into the interaction between the individual and the law.

Responses to Discrimination

People who experience discrimination appear to have a range of political and legal actions open to them. What they in fact choose to do is shaped in part by how they perceive social reality and how they define their own interests in situations of conflict. In general, people's responses to discrimination are problematic, and their actions constrained, so that the important question is why only an exceptional few who perceive they have experienced discrimination achieve successful resolution of their problems.

The initial source of data for this study was a household survey designed to measure the incidence of civil disputes. In the survey, conducted by the Civil Litigation Research Project (CLRP) in 1980, a sample of 560 discrimination claims was obtained from a sample of approximately five thousand households. Respondents were asked if they had experienced "illegal or unfair treatment" because of their "race, age, sex, handicaps, union membership, or other things."[10] In this way, it was possible to obtain a sample of discrimination grievances that had not reached courts or public agencies. Preliminary analysis indicated that approximately half of the aggrieved individuals did not make a claim to the other party, nearly two-thirds did nothing further to rectify their perceived mistreatment, and only a very small percentage had achieved successful resolution of their claims.[11] Discrimination grievances had a significantly lower rate of escalation into court cases than other civil matters such as contract disputes and landlord-tenant problems. The size of the gap indicates the more problematic relationship between victims and the law in discrimination compared to other civil cases. My study began with the anticipation that to bring the complaint into the realm of public action forced victims to encounter deeper and more encompassing conflicts of racial, gender, and social identity than complaints arising from relationships defined by legal roles (e.g., landlord and tenant). What accounts for the apparent acceptance of defeat among those who experience discriminatory treatment? Why is it unlikely that those who experience discrimination will take their claims to courts or other legal channels?

In the CLRP survey, individuals who perceived they had experienced discrimination but had made no protest were prompted to explain their decision by being asked, "Why didn't you complain?" In response, participants denied the worthiness of their own interests in comparison to their opponents' (table 1). Some respondents accounted for their inaction in terms of the harm their opponent could impose on them (responses 5, 8, 9 in table 1). Others acknowledged they should have done something, yet either blamed themselves for not pursuing the dispute or accepted the inevitability of the situation (responses 1, 2, 3, 4,

One / Responses to "Why Didn't You Complain?"

Coded Responses*	No. of Responses (Percentage)
1. It would do no good/end results the same/a way of life	35 (19.9)
2. Not worth it/not a major problem	18 (10.2)
3. Need to solve the problem immediately/situation easily replaceable	17 (9.7)
4. Gave up/I don't know why I didn't complain/I'm easy going	17 (9.7)
5. Fear of retaliation or being known as a troublemaker	16 (9.1)
6. Don't know who to complain to	14 (8.0)
7. Could not prove/no evidence	13 (7.4)
8. Avoid dealing with them in the future	12 (6.8)
9. Don't want to cause trouble	9 (5.1)
10. Excessive time or cost	9 (5.1)
11. Rules cannot be changed	8 (4.6)
12. Other	8 (4.6)

* Open-ended responses were coded into these twelve categories. These questions (tables 1 and 2) were administered to a subsample of the total number of people experiencing discrimination problems.

11 in table 1). The explanations focused on an interpretation of immediate circumstances rather than norms or rights; for example, the expense of legal action or the inability to prove discriminatory motives (responses 6, 7, 10 in table 1).[12]

A more complete picture is imparted by these individuals' responses to questions about the outcome of their dispute (table 2). The responses to the inquiry "What was the final outcome?" indicate that even for those who seek redress there is, in fact, little chance of success. In 61 percent of the cases (responses 1 and 2 in table 2) no satisfaction of the claim was achieved. Many who made claims received no response from their opponents; hence, they stopped pursuing the claim or were resigned to an implicit stand-off. Some people resolved the issue by finding another situation (18.5 percent, response 3 in table 2); the dispute ended when they left their job, housing, school, or other situation voluntarily or involuntarily. A much smaller percentage of respondents' claims (11.3 percent, response 6 in table 2) were fully satisfied by the other party. The experiences of this sample of individuals show that the other party rarely responds satisfactorily to a claim of discrimination; usually the matter is resolved by the victim's resignation to the perceived injustice.

The model of legal protection would suggest that the failure of persons to use the law stems from the victims' inability to serve their own needs: lack of information and knowledge about their rights and their

Two / Responses to "What Was the Final Outcome—How Did the Matter End?"

Coded Responses	No. of Responses (Percentage)
1. Nothing was done/dropped the claim/stand-off with opponent	77 (34.7)
2. Left situation/fired from job/flunked out of school	59 (26.6)
3. Found another situation (job, housing, etc.)	41 (18.5)
4. Satisfied eventually (problem took care of itself, received what was wanted not directly due to claim)	11　(5.0)
5. Partially satisfied	5　(2.3)
6. Claim satisfied (by other party)	25 (11.3)
7. Received formal apology	4　(1.8)

limited resources for using legal channels. But these persons were not rejected by unresponsive agencies, deterred by the cost and unavailability of lawyers, or barred from pursuing legal claims by technicalities. Although the anticipation of these factors played a role in their decision making, they did not take action primarily because they legitimized their own defeat. For the most part, the problem is never conceptualized in terms of public action. In this universe of discrimination problems far removed from legal forums, the labeling of acts as discriminatory and the eventual deflation of the conflict by apology or self-blame serve as coping mechanisms for suppressing burgeoning discontent.

The resolution of these conflicts without direct confrontation between the victims of discrimination and their adversaries amounts to surrender to systematic procedures that perpetuate inequalities. The barriers to making claims are not legal technicalities, for most of these cases never get far enough for the written law to be a factor. These people do not take action because they assume that their complaints will not be taken seriously. They choose to submit to the practices of employers, landlords, and others, rather than demanding satisfaction.

One function of procedural justice is to give meaningful expression to individual rights. In a democracy, "rites of justice" manifest a society's respect for each citizen's individuality.[13] It is problematic, however, whether the ideology of antidiscrimination serves to reaffirm the worth of people encountering social prejudice or whether it contributes to a distortion of their interests. The examination of a large number of disputes from the Civil Litigation Research Project survey and other studies indicates that for most claimants defeat is likely if not inevitable.

These data reveal a general pattern of response, but provide limited insight into the social psychological situation. More adequate explanations for legal action or inaction are derived from an examination of their responses in the context of their lives: the social exchange between authorities and those discriminated against, the social and psychological mechanisms that stifle conflict, and the role of legal ideology in influencing individual choice. I sought these explanations through intensive interviewing that elucidated the victims' views of social reality and their perceptions of alternative courses of action.[14]

I selected a subsample of eighteen persons in Milwaukee and Los Angeles for in-depth interviewing.[15] The format of the interviews was unstructured but directed at probing for interpretations of the discrimination incident, people's attitudes about themselves and their social status, and their justifications for their beliefs and actions.[16] The interviews were conducted from April to October 1982. Each face-to-face interview was two to four hours long. The participants in the interviews were representative of those affected by the social inequalities and the pattern of discrimination in American society: six black and Hispanic women, nine white women, and three black and American Indian men.[17]

The Study of Legal Consciousness

The voices of victims cannot be heard unless the researcher listens from a vantage point that gives meaning and authority to their words. There are two methodological questions that must be addressed: From what standpoint do we evaluate the self-reports of individuals involved in legal conflicts? What understanding can be gained from their ideas, expressions, and dialogues? The answers to these questions will help us account for the victims' defeat and self-blame without losing sight of the potential for social change.

The conventional perspective that describes individual response to law takes on the polarized viewpoint of legal authority vis-à-vis its subjects. The laws are created, interpreted, and executed for subjects who are ordered, dominated, and ruled. The language of the law is the language of command; law is power imposed from above. Those subject to legal authority are seen as either rejecting or bolstering the law's legitimacy. The layperson's attitude toward the law is usually of interest to the legal reformer only as a measure of the level of support for the legal system. When public opinion is surveyed, the underlying concern is, Does faith in the moral efficacy of the law sustain its legitimacy? Research influenced by this polarized imagery of legal authorities and their subjects has not uncovered a "legal consciousness" apart from authoritative discourse on law. This inquiry into legal consciousness will (1) suggest that in a variety of ways the expressions of those subjected to legal control are interpreted only through the eyes of the powerful, and (2) convey the outlines of a perspective that gives validity to those expressions.

From what standpoint does mass consciousness constitute valid knowledge of legal phenomena? I begin to examine this question in terms of its intellectual history. Karl Mannheim in *Ideology and Utopia* characterizes the modern epistemological and sociological point of view as validated by the "knowing subject."[18] In Mannheim's account, this epistemological orientation is attributed to the demise of the certainty of the medieval unitary world view and the rise of the foundation of knowledge based upon an individualistic and psychological understanding of one's existence.

This attempt to find meaning in terms of the genesis of the subject, however, limited the observation of meaningful experience to the individual. Yet, the emergence of a more sociological understanding in which thought was constituted in events interpreted as collective and social experiences failed to provide a more adequate foundation of knowledge. Both the demise of the unitary world view and the recognized plurality of "thoughtstyles" created the intellectual crisis that has given rise to the modern conception of ideology. Mannheim writes, "There is implicit in the word 'ideology' the insight that in certain situations the collective unconscious of certain groups obscures the real condition of society both to itself and to others and thereby stabilizes it."[19] Thus, the discovery of the social consciousness and ideology emerges from its own intellectual dilemma, the search for the basis of judging the truth and value of our thinking.

Synonymous with this construction of the social-situational world view was the tendency to view the process of social discovery as the "unmasking" of unconscious motivations. Mass consciousness is "distorted" or "ideological" when the realities of the social situation are concealed by thinking in "inappropriate categories."[20] False consciousness poses an irreconcilable dilemma for the foundation of knowledge or the search for a "true" reality. The reality of the subject does not allow for a social viewpoint distinct from the ideology of those in authority.

When the problem of ideology is raised in terms of the status of knowledge of legal actors, we also find it difficult to distinguish between the authority of the lawmakers and the mass public.[21] The rationalization of law in modern society strengthens ideological control,[22] such that the elite have a pervasive role in the shaping of public attitudes about law and in filtering access to legal channels. Those who have studied the repressive aspects of legal ideology, such as Lukács and other Marxist interpreters of the law, see this formalization or rationalization of the law as creating a structure of legal images that makes law remote from material existence. They find that the rationalization of modern law gives the appearance of rigidity in the face of a reality of continuous change and conflict. An incoherent body of law appears general, unified, and formally logical, creating a pretense about the true structure of social relations.[23] Once resigned to the state of domination under the conditions of the modern legal system, citizens reinforce this domination through submission to the directives and interpretations of legal authorities.

There are numerous elaborations of the preceding account of the role of legal ideology in structuring mass consciousness. The problem emerges as a question of legal domination, which is, again, the problem of giving a meaningful voice to the subject apart from the rule of law. The impasse, put in terms of a political strategy, is the need to tap a source of creativity that can change the human condition, to find a strategy to liberate individuals from stultifying realities created by political and legal repression. Marcuse, whose work takes this question as a starting point, frames the concern in the following way:

> In the last analysis, the question of what are true and false needs must be answered by the individuals themselves, but only in the last analysis; that is, if and when they are free to give their own answer. As long as they are kept incapable of being autonomous, as long as they are indoctrinated and manipulated (down to their very instincts), their answer to this question cannot be taken as their own....[O]ur revulsion [of a tribunal arrogating the right to decide]...does not do away with the question: how can the people who have been the object of effective and productive domination by themselves create the conditions of freedom?[24]

This question arises in many guises. It is the question of the existence of freedom apart from domination. One optimistic line of response that is the focus of the following examination of research method is to scrutinize the role of ideology as an instrument of total control over people's lives.

Legal Power

Michel Foucault's account of law and social control provides a framework for interpreting people's responses to law that does not rely on the polarized image of authority and subjects. Law is an instrument of power rather than a reflection of the social or economic sphere or a "mask for power." Foucault states: "Law is neither the truth of power nor its alibi. It is an instrument of power which is at once complex and partial."[25] Law has both a repressive and a facilitative side. In its repressive form, legal control is coordinated with nonlegal mechanisms. The coercive function of modern penal systems, for example, depends upon the conjunction of juridical (or sovereign) and disciplinary forms of power (e.g., the judge's power extends beyond formal sentencing power to an assessment of the criminal's normality and the delegation of authority to numerous psychiatric supervisors).[26] The facilitative side of law enhances the coordination of legal strategies by the state. For example, the failure of the prison to improve recidivism rates (despite its justifications based on intentions of reform) is neither a social contradiction nor a failure of the ideal put into practice. Foucault explains, "[P]enalty does not simply 'check' illegalities; it 'differentiates' them, it provides them with a general 'economy.'"[27] Prisons create a particular type of illegality, delinquency, that is "politically and economically less dangerous" than unchecked illegalities (e.g., banditry or mass political disruption).

Law is not seen as a repressive tool but as a form of power implemented through legal institutions and professionals. The argument is clearly put: "We must cease once and for all to describe power in negative terms: it excludes, it represses, it censors, it abstracts, it masks, it conceals. In fact, power produces; it produces reality; it produces domains of objects and rituals of truth."[28] Legal power creates a reality through the production of scientific knowledge and disciplinary institutions.

This view of power and law in society is the foundation of Foucault's analysis of the role of ideology in structuring mass consciousness. His work questions both the conception of a "global ideology" and the strategy of ideological demystification. Foucault asserts, with sleight of hand, that what takes place in social practice is both "more and less than ideology." It is less than ideology, because forms of law and power impose their authority without an ideological superstructure. Power is exercised through "subtle mechanisms" that "evolve, organise, and put into circulation a knowledge, or rather apparatuses of knowledge, which are not ideological constructs."[29] These mechanisms of power are illustrated by the metaphor of the panopticon, an architectural design of a prison, where the structure of the prison apparatus imposes control that is indeterminable, individualizing, and all-pervasive. Power reaches deeply into the lives controlled by its mechanisms, not tangentially through ideological constructs. Ideologies, or more specifically ideological constructs, are marginal in the everyday process of oppression.

Foucault's conception of law and ideology moves us away from the conventional view of antidiscrimination law as a command directed at perpetrators to recognition of the law as a form of knowledge and power that influences its subjects (the victims of discrimination). This raises the question of how law exercises its authority on victims and produces the victims' views of themselves and their situation.

Strategies of Method

Methodology creates its own orientation to the study of legal consciousness. The desire to implement a methodology that seeks to explore the influence of ideology on individual consciousness reflects a particular political orientation to the subject. At the most obvious level, the desire to talk with one's subjects, as opposed to reading the laws that govern them, is a challenge to the elitism of social research. A direct way to explore the discrepancy between elite and mass consciousness is to enlarge the nonauthoritative sources of the data base.

Intensive interviewing (distinct from participant observation, which is employed in many anthropological studies of law in society) is a particularly obtrusive form of interaction between the researcher and the subject. The interviewer is aggressive, challenging the person's responses in order to bring out the full extent of her or his understanding and to make obvious the internal contradictions in the subject's positions. Even the researcher who approaches the situation with neutrality (to the extent of not offering personal opinions) is involved in a discussion that calls into question the researcher's legitimacy and purpose when intervening in the lives of the respondents.[30]

Professional-client interactions involve ritualistic behavior aimed at affirming the expertise of the professional. The "confidence game" in the attorney's office, for example, convinces the clients of the worth of professional services.[31] The social science interviewer and the willing subject are also involved in a confidence game that raises serious questions about the sincerity of the inquiry. The sycophantic nature of the research experience is made evident by the one-sided exchange of ideas. Hypocrisy is also built into the ritual of research: unlike counselors, lawyers, doctors, and other professionals who know that the "subject" has sought them out, researchers have chosen their clientele. The ritual of providing a service does not provide reassurance.

To make sense of the interview experience, researchers need a clear understanding of the knowledge sought from their subjects;[32] otherwise they may lose the richness of the interviewees' accounts and their own reactions. The interviews become ritualistic when there are unresolved questions about the authority of the respondents' accounts. Are respondents nonfictional characters in a novel-like presentation of social life? Are they repositories of "valid" knowledge about social life distinct from elite ideology? Or is the researcher actually engaged in "shaking out" of the subjects a level of false consciousness or attempting to make sense of an otherwise inscrutable working of their minds?

These are important and difficult questions; they find their most satisfactory solution in the context of the objectives of the particular study. In these interviews, I am not searching for amorphous references to ideological predispositions; instead, the focus is on the strategies used by individuals involved in legal conflict. I attempt to transform the act of interviewing from ritual into meaningful exchange by formulating objectives that bring together the knowledge of the respondent with a perspective on legal ideology. In this study of discrimination grievances, the four objectives of interviewing are:

1. to provide meaningful interpretations of conflict in the context of individual lives;
2. to analyze the structure of rationalizations;

3. to discover when and how law enters personal spheres; and
4. to understand power at the extreme points of its exercise.

Providing meaningful interpretations of conflict in the context of individual lives. Individuals provide a guide to the realities and contingencies that influence life choices. They must reconcile roles and life objectives (family, work, conflicting information, etc.) to deal with conflict and then use these reflections to make choices. Ralf Dahrendorf cites as the failure of conflict theory its formality and inability to say something about the substance of social life.[33] His operationalization of the concept "life chances" links individual development to social structures. The concept of life chances "provides an important bridge between an understanding of society which emphasizes the structural qualities of things social...and a normative theory of society which emphasizes individual liberty."[34] The concept integrates the analysis of role behavior, formal rules, and theories of social change with the substratum of the motives, intentions, interests, needs, and expectations expressed in individual lives. Life chances are not measures of objective conditions; they are probabilities of obtaining wants or needs, or probabilities that events will occur that satisfy those desires.

The concept of life chances raises questions that bring together the structure of law and the opportunities of an actor in a given situation. It raises the question that orients my inquiry: *What is the probability that the belief in the possession of a "right" will further the interests of a person engaged in a discrimination conflict?* An important premise of this book, therefore, is that neither the potentialities nor the troubles deriving from social conflict can be fully understood outside of the changes in an individual life.

The focus on life chances prevents imposition of a rigid dichotomy between the personal and psychological and the social and political domains. The complexities found in the contingencies of everyday situations and "psychological" motivations are drawn together with the analysis of the structure of authority and legal institutions. Specifically, in terms of discrimination conflicts I find that the discrimination incident is not isolated from struggles for survival and opportunities in the course of everyday life, and that persons respond to discrimination in ways that are determined by the larger societal pressures constraining personal and social identities.

Analyzing the structure of rationalizations. People's descriptions of conflict involve rationalizations, as does the presentation of almost all justifications for social behavior. Rationalizations are important because people act upon them. The term *rationalization* is being used in this context to refer to artifacts of communication spoken by those who experience conditions of powerlessness. It is a form of communication that reveals both conscious and unconscious acceptance of limitations on individual choice. Rationalizations are loosely referred to as "data," because they illuminate the ways in which the powerful influence social behavior. The content of rationalizations is a source of data about conflicts, because it explains why alternative courses of action are unlikely.

Bruno Bettelheim explains how rationalizations offered by prisoners in the extreme situation of the Nazi concentration camp justified their construction of a building for the Gestapo. When controversies arose over whether the building was necessary, "they rationalized that the new Germany would have to use these buildings. When it was pointed out that a revolution would have to destroy the fortresses of the Gestapo, old prisoners would retire to the general statement that one ought to do well any job one has to do."[35]

Bettelheim illustrates how rationalizations operate in extreme conditions. His example demonstrates that rationalizations are created when actions are incongruent with beliefs, and that rationalizations reveal how tensions are resolved in the minds of victims when they are given no opportunity to resist. Rationalizations are central to the way victims of discrimination describe their experience. Many respondents actually pride themselves on their ability to rationalize; rationalizations get them through a "bad situation" and make them feel "in control." In cases of discrimination, both the types of rationalizations and their effects on behavior offer important insights into why people tolerate conditions they perceive to be unjust and how existing inequalities are maintained.

Discovering when and how law enters personal spheres.   Law intervenes in people's lives. When beliefs about law, legal concepts, and issues of rights and wrongs become salient to a social conflict, the "legal theme" influences communication and perceptions of the incident. For example, once an individual perceives the nature of the conflict as discriminatory, the situation is transformed by the introduction of the law even if the parties do not speak to lawyers or bring the case to a legal forum. Niklas Luhmann refers to this process as legal "thematization" and is interested in how the introduction of law influences the communication process for the participants involved.[36] Luhmann's model merges social situational (macro) and interpersonal (micro) levels of analysis. The model describes how law imposed from above modifies communicative interactions, not only by its content, but by the restructuring of the conflict to facilitate a legal resolution.

The intervention of law changes the balance of power within social relationships. The introduction of legal themes may influence behavior at all stages of the conflict—from its initiation to its resolution. When one or both of the parties invokes the law, this tactic can encourage compliance with preexisting rules but also may stabilize, destabilize, destroy, or facilitate the relationship between the parties or bring uncertainty, coherence, or closure to the conflict. The restructuring of communication patterns may be unwelcome to the parties; they may view the law as a presence in their lives they would choose to avoid. Legal themes may also unsettle the balance of power between the parties engaged in conflict. It may appear in written law that the injured party benefits, but in practice the intervention of legal themes may imperil the party with the weakest social support outside of the law.

Understanding power at the extreme points of its exercise.   This involves observing interactions between authority and subject, leader and led, or oppressor and victim. We gain insights into the exercise of authority, legal power, acquiescence, and the workings of the instruments of the law by investigating the actual process of give and take between the weak and the strong. The psychological weapons of paternalism, fear and tyranny, alienation, and conformity can be seen not only as ideological forces or constructs but as ingredients that transform, bind, and control personal relationships. This microsociological approach may best describe the actual workings of domination and submission.

Law exercises its power by less obvious means than can be discerned from formal and visible decision making in court. From Foucault's perspective, the study of power, and therefore law, should not be concerned with the "regulated and legitimate forms of power in their central locations, with the general mechanisms through which they operate, and the continual effects of these."[37] An alternative view of power, at "its extremities," diverts attention from the institutional apparatus of the state and the courts. Power is located "at the extreme points of its exercise, where it is always less legal in character."[38] But it would be incorrect to infer from this statement that "central locations" are diversionary. The interests of the state in punishment, hospitals, and the family (to use Foucault's examples), or in court cases, are not absent. Macrosocial and economic forces and the power of the state prevail over social life in their "external visages." The external visage of state power shapes and defines interpersonal relations, professional and everyday discourses, and the setting and movement of social life. The state does not control less, it controls more effectively through intervening in the core of people's lives. The power imposed by legal doctrine and institutions may delude, not because they are disguised as powerful, but because the illusion created by official doctrine hides the realities of how and by what means the powerful control society.[39]

Power relations materalize in their external visages in the everyday discourses of the powerful and the powerless. Foucault views the master-slave dialectic (love for the master creating fear of violation and guilt) as an empty analogy because all acts of power by the oppressed are seen as transgressions. This image of the subject is rooted in the modern condition in which the disciplinary system individualizes its victims. The victim is not the object of domination when power is viewed as relational; power is never possessed like a commodity. Individuals are "vehicles of power," therefore; subordination is not a quality or state of the subject, but is constituted in the subject in terms of a fluid power relation. Domination may be achieved, for example, through the acceptance of legal constructs in everyday discourse.

Conclusion

This strategy of method provides concrete examples of how the subject's knowledge can be meaningfully understood in the interpretation of legal disputes. It is a strategy, depending upon the creativity of its empirical realization, that can offer a different perspective on the role of both the powerful and the powerless.

This work is motivated by the desire to make social science research more responsive to the problem of social oppression and the stultifying reality of everyday life. In it I attempt to address the question of how individuals formulate their own interests, and I assume that these interests are constrained by perceptions of one's social reality. I hope that the interpretation of these social realities can create a liberating vision of alternative possibilities.[40]

The characters that will appear here have expressed an inner life that is most often disregarded by social scientists. As Marcuse states, the essence of art is the refusal to accept fact.[41] To recognize the complex social construction of their life worlds, I have had to distance myself from my interviewees' acceptance of fact and to begin to create a world with the potentialities of fiction. This process first will involve presenting these persons' situations in a way that can convey the brutality, fear, and disappointment that pervade their lives.[42] A form of analysis which could not express these feelings would do violence to the meaning of the interviews. Second, it is important to appreciate how the aesthetic form of a conflict situation determines the outcome. In particular, legal conflict, despite its distance from the courtroom, often becomes ritualized. The conflict is restructured by the symbolic forms of the law; ambiguous situations are transformed into legal events. The language of the law, with its jargon and predictable form and content, may contribute to the predetermination of unsuccessful outcomes in discrimination disputes.

I attempt to offer a convincing explanation of a configuration of events that integrates their social, historical, and psychological facets: explanation becomes a gestalt exercise. Capturing the interviewees' social realities requires an appreciation of the literal interpretations of their accounts, as one would sympathize with the difficulties experienced by a friend. Yet at the analysis stage, it requires me to distance myself from their experiences, in order to reconcile and explain their contradictory impressions and reactions. The distance also makes possible the depiction of an ideological perspective that can explain the creation of the "factual" world views of these persons. It is from this description of their world view that this study derives its theme: that antidiscrimination law serves to reinforce the victimization of its "beneficiaries."

Three / The Historical Roots of Antidiscrimination Ideology

The faith in law as an instrument for eradicating discrimination is rooted in the conventional history of race law. The civil rights society is seen as the legacy of social progress that has vindicated the original constitutional intent to provide every citizen with free and equal treatment under law.[1] Since the renewal of the commitment to these principles in the Thirteenth and Fourteenth amendments, this progressive course is seen as the continuous, but gradual, route to a more harmonious society. The conventional historical framework centers on the role of public law in promoting social change and defines the purpose of legal intervention as serving the interest of national unity and facilitating the growth of individual freedom.

When this view of the role of law takes form in concrete social relations, it reinforces certain explanations of the origins and causes of racial oppression. The historical foundations of social consciousness define the identity of the victim, assign blame and responsibility, and designate appropriate solutions. Thus, when blacks, women, and other disadvantaged groups embrace the law as a means of achieving social justice, the law also grabs hold of them by imposing a vision of history that determines their potential courses of action. In this chapter I explore how people's views of the law are historically determined and question the received wisdom about the history of law reform. In particular, I bring doubt on the assumption that antidiscrimination policies were originally conceived of, or can be continued to be employed, as a tactic for political liberation. Relying on the insights from the previous chapter, this reconstructed history acknowledges both the facilitative and the repressive purposes of race law. This requires looking behind the grand design of public law to the effects of private law and the consequences of legal rules on interpersonal relations.

Transformation of Ideologies

During periods of major crisis, ideologies emerge that provide a new orientation to the social world.[2] The creation of new ideologies not only makes the transformed social order comprehensible, it brings about new instruments of power that legitimate the reconstructed system. The Foucaultian insight is that old forms of domination do not disappear at major historical discontinuities; they are reborn as more effective instruments of power. This transformation in forms of domination is illustrated by the Beccarian revolution in criminal law, the birth of modern strategies of deterrence and punishment. This "revolution" replaced a prereform system of discretionary power with the Enlightenment ideal of criminal law that was guided by moderation and utilitarian premises. These great reforms were prepared from within the system, because the inconsistencies in the application of judicial discretion created a "bad economy of power," and the forms of justice as terror had the potential to provoke insidious rebellion.[3] The new forms of punishment employed the "corrective techniques" of medical and legal professionals and supervision, both inside and outside the prison, to isolate and control "delinquents."[4] In the new system, criminal law began its unending efforts at reform—of the legal institution, and of the legal subject. The modern system of punishment set up a self-perpetuating cycle of reform; efficiency, effectiveness, and most of all, reform, became the defining purposes of criminal law.

In Foucault's analysis, the transformation from a violent and unstable system to a more "humane" system represented new forms of social control that depend on the labeling and treatment of potentially disruptive classes.[5] The analogy raises questions about whether many social reforms are intended to fail, so that consequently institutions may justify the reassertion of their authority over classes of "undesirables"; further, the continued need for treatment of "delinquents" or racial groups perpetuates their low status. In American civil law, the doctrine of antidiscrimination has set into motion a process of reforming the conditions of racial oppression and has classified certain groups as beneficiaries of these laws. These doctrines descended from the law of slavery and may have assumed, in part, the role of maintaining control over the new class of citizens. This comparison between the pre–Civil War legal system and the post–Civil War emergence of the model of legal protection emphasizes the modification of private legal mechanisms that regulated the former slaves' actions and the shifts in the exercise of legal power that led to the formation of current legal strategies.

The Birth of Antidiscrimination Law, 1860–1900

The Civil War marked drastic changes in social, political and economic structures that were the basis of a "constitutional revolution."[6] The Civil War was a revolutionary crisis in a political and economic sense; for example, Barrington Moore, Jr., describes the war as the "last revolutionary offensive on the part of a bourgeois capitalist democracy."[7] The "prerevolutionary" South was capitalist, but not bourgeois and urban. And fundamentally, a system of democratic equality contradicted the Southern lifestyle. The cause and consequences of the Civil War thus reached beyond the moral issue of slavery to the problem of affirming a system of democratic capitalism in the South.

The pre–Civil War slave society was characterized by both severe and explosive forms of domination. The institution of slavery emerged in American society unchecked by pressures from other institutions. The growth of slavery as an institution was encouraged by unmitigated capitalist development, the lack of controls over the physical discipline of slaves, and noninterference by the church.[8] Slave law evolved unbounded by these constraints and resulted in a body of doctrine that rationalized, simplified, and made logical the inconsistencies between the institution of slavery and democratic ideals.[9]

The pre–Civil War slavery issue was morally explosive. As a subject of political discussion, slavery "had almost assumed the character of the original sin."[10] The issue of slavery was cast in terms of moral severity by both the Northern abolitionists and the Southern proslavery factions. The defense of slavery amounted to the defense of the entire Southern way of life.[11] This explosiveness was also found in the master-slave relationship, where any transgression against the master could be interpreted as a threat to the structure of authority in the Southern plantation.[12] The conflicts that arose over slave conditions were the roots of emerging violence. When proslavery and antislavery debates led to a violent confrontation on the Senate floor, it symbolized to many Northerners "the aggressions of Slave Power. . . .[and that] [v]iolence began to replace legal and political processes."[13]

Most significantly, the slavery issue became a threat to national authority. A series of prewar compromises failed to ease the tension of competing national interests. The issue of slavery was nationalized by the Supreme Court under Chief Justice Taney, to the extent that the Court recognized that the problem of slavery required national uniformity, but the direction and implementation of national authority were left to be resolved.[14]

At the symbolic level, the post–Civil War slave question was embodied in a great moral commitment: the Emancipation Proclamation promised a biracial society, where the legal terms of equality were consistent with political democracy and a system of economic capitalism that replaced master-slave oppression. And the moral commitment of the Thirteenth Amendment was unbounded, freeing citizens from all forms of servitude.

The symbolic commitment to equality was, however, immediately circumvented by the enactment of the Black Codes in the former slave states. The Black Codes acknowledged the free status of the former slaves, granting them the right to buy and sell personal property, the right to marry, freedom of movement, and the right to testify in court. But they also entailed a list of civil disabilities, recreating many of the restrictions found in slave law.[15] These laws provided a separate criminal code for black citizens and devices for state control. The Black Codes can be seen as the first experiment in the redesign of legality that institutionalized injustice and prejudice in state constitutions and laws. But the codes were an unsuccessful experiment (their rescission was brought on by political pressure) because they were thinly disguised efforts to reenact the substance of slavery.[16]

The second phase of Reconstruction policies had two major effects on the nature of legal power: it brought a fundamental shift in political power with the expansion of federal judicial authority and preserved the economics of slavery through devising economic forms of servitude. The structural expansion of judicial power was brought about by the reorganization acts of the 1860s and the creation of the intermediate courts of appeal. This expansion has been described as a "silent, almost imperceptible revolution...in the bases of federal judicial power."[17] Far from playing a passive role during the Reconstruction era, the courts set a pattern that circumvented the Fourteenth Amendment's national authority and condoned repressive state legislation—in effect, giving constitutional sanction to segregation. A study of post–Civil War cases in lower federal courts before *Plessy v. Ferguson* indicates a continuity between antebellum law and new policies of social segregation of the races. The evidence shows that judges examined the actual conditions of black accommodations in civil rights cases, but ruled that the legal right to equality did not extend beyond "separate but equal."[18]

The "Negro question" became part of a strategy for enlarging the base of federal control. One historian contends that the purposes of court actions did not extend to any immediate interest in improving the condition of former slaves:

> The concern for the Negro...[as a] constitutional and legal problem... more properly might be viewed as a by-product of the Republicans' conscious and well-articulated desires to reconstruct the nation—that is, to reconstruct the nation in order to insure constitutional and political hegemony for the physically dominant section and, correspondingly, to expand the authority and policy function of the federal government, which that section would control.[19]

Within the Republican strategy were the "seeds of failure";[20] the failure of the court's strategy for promoting equality, yet the success of establishing federal judicial authority.

Reconstruction-era legal authority established a method of federal intervention that preceded present-day antidiscrimination strategies. As the grand design of Reconstruction policies was met with increasing obstructions and violence, the protection of the black citizen was delegated to the courts and legal enforcement. This marked the end of the duty of Reconstruction politicians to scrutinize the results of civil rights protection and the beginning of the reliance on legal procedures, which were viewed as effective remedies. The moral purpose of Reconstruction was lost to a faith in legal effectiveness.[21] The black citizen then became the invisible beneficiary of the law. Harold Hyman and William Wiecek write:

> The fact that the death of slavery was indeed a product of wartime expediency clouded the history of the emancipation in the 1860s and obscures its characteristics even now. Clearly, by the 1880s, white America lost the sense of moral anger and escalating common national purpose that brought it to emancipation and then to the protection of civil rights. . . .That sense lost, *the Negro, its initial and primary beneficiary. . ., became all but invisible.*[22]

The movement toward legal instrumentalism and its tenets of judicial self-restraint further removed the judicial function from the actual implementation of legal protection for blacks.[23]

During this time of federal expansion of judicial authority, slavery was economically metamorphosed into forms of involuntary servitude, or peonage. The post–Civil War labor system was an "unpatterned blend of illiteracy, law, constraints, and violence."[24] The strength and power of the system was its confusing combination of contractual obligation and violent control. The post–Civil War labor system was built upon the structure of chattel slavery; its techniques included concealing the full extent of emancipation and instituting more violent forms of domination.

Postslavery control was achieved largely through law—through contracts with terms resembling slavery, vagrancy statutes, and criminal laws.[25] The legal structure defined and facilitated the system of peonage. These private law (primarily contracts) and criminal law mechanisms reestablished economic slavery in the South during Reconstruction, and it continued well into the twentieth century. The most common form of such legislation was found in "enticement laws," enacted in ten Southern states from 1865 to 1867, that maintained the former master-slave relationship by penalizing those who would entice black workers from both implied and explicit contracts with employers. Also, "contract-enforcement" statutes were aimed directly at regulating the former slaves through coercive, and by the 1880s more subtle, forced labor agreements.[26] The result was a flexible and adaptable system that "blended slavery and freedom" in a manner that enabled white Southerners to exercise control over black labor while maintaining the appearance of legitimacy.[27]

In summary, the post–Civil War legal system constituted a revision of strategy for control over black citizens. The realities of the economic and political situation of the new citizens subverted the moral pronouncements about their freedom. Immediately, Reconstruction policies began the retrenchment from the promise of emancipation and the Thirteenth and Fourteenth amendments. The post–Civil War legal system emerged, at first, undisturbed in basic design from slave law, through the enactment of Black Codes. Next, two forms of legality predominated during the Reconstruction era. First, legality became interwoven with the economic system, creating a patchwork of legalized means of restricting the former slaves' freedom. The role of the law in constraining the freedom of black persons was less visible, in the sense that it was localized and the liabilities were instituted through private law, yet the law played an active role in the preservation of economic domination. Second, the law assumed the role of "passive" protection, meaning that the courts asserted broader authority while withdrawing from the responsibility for enforcement. The faith in legal effectiveness affirmed federal authority. The protection of civil rights after 1865 increasingly became a response to state restrictions on a free person's status, rather than focusing on rights that allowed freedom to contract, licensing in trade, and other primarily economic rights in a person's state and community (which was the pre–Civil War view of civil liberties).[28] From the Reconstruction experience the modern view of legal rights through federal protection was established—the view that (1) legal procedures are effective instruments of social restraint and change; (2) civil rights are dynamic and not static guarantees; and (3) the nature of civil rights at a given time depends upon close scrutiny of the situation affecting rights.[29]

The shift in political, social, and economic conditions coincident with the Civil War marked the end of the invisibility of the slavery issue in the American democratic imagination. It marked the beginning, however, of the invisibility of the "protected minority" in equal protection doctrine. Antidiscrimination strategy found its roots in Reconstruction policy, yet it remained dormant or circumvented until the social movements of the twentieth century. Then the courts activated the equal protection doctrine in response to the rise of mass, discontent.

The failure of Reconstruction legality to set the course for greater equality and freedom for blacks cannot be seen simply as the result of limited moral purpose and political circumvention. The structure of these laws did not provide the newly created citizens with affirmative civil rights or strategies of enforcement that could initiate social change.

Civil Rights as a Social Movement, 1950–1972

When twentieth-century activism emerged, many black leaders relied on the rhetorical evocation of the Constitution to express the moral superiority of their cause. The romanticized version of the civil rights movement gives more credit to the symbolic force of the law than to the people who dedicated their lives to the fight against racism. This perspective on social history is supported by the assumption that there is harmony between legal strategies and organized activism—or, more precisely, that activism follows in the wake of litigation. Yet, retrospective evaluation of the movement reveals that civil rights activism was in many ways fundamentally incompatible with the legalistic currents of the movement. Beginning in the fifties and continuing into the early seventies, however, these two strains attempted to coexist. These tensions within the movement eventually led to the demise of the social protest phase and the emergence of a new era of passivity.[30]

The National Association for the Advancement of Colored People (NAACP) was the strongest black civil rights organization during the first half of the twentieth century. Its subsequently limited role in mass social protest was preordained by the group's history and organization. The part played by the NAACP was hindered by its inability to achieve a mass power base. The founders of the group were elite black and white Northerners, and its local membership bases throughout the nation were never able to enlist much more than 2 percent of the black population.[31] More importantly, the organization had specialized goals to further the advancement of black people, objectives that were to be carried out through bureaucratic organization and litigation strategies. These objectives made the NAACP the focus of attack by the early leaders of the more radical Student Nonviolent Coordinating Committee (SNCC). SNCC's James Lawson criticized the NAACP's emphasis on "fund-raising and court action" in place of other efforts to empower the victims of "racial evil."[32] Even leaders of the more moderate Southern Christian Leadership Conference (SCLC) believed that the NAACP's expenditures of energy and money on test cases led to little progress in fighting racial domination.[33] Although NAACP members were involved in the early sit-ins and other protest activities, the organization was committed to change within the system and was generally unreceptive to alternative tactics that may have threatened its bureaucratic organization.[34]

The emerging activism, however, had its roots in the South and drew upon the strengths of traditional black institutions. The strongest organization was the SCLC, which drew its energies from the charismatic leadership of Dr. Martin Luther King, Jr., and others. Yet the SCLC also quickly gained strength because its civil rights campaign was based upon the preexisting resources of the black church.[35]

The period of black activism in the South grew from exceptional circumstances. The early stages of the movement were focused on the forms of racism, including segregation and the denial of other citizenship rights, that had continually humiliated and degraded blacks in situations of everyday life. The battle against the most visible signs of racist domination encouraged the black community to defend its basic survival and dignity and introduced the struggle to the white community in terms of goals consistent with democratic pluralism. The concentration and isolation of black neighborhoods and the strong communal ties that developed in response to economic oppression served to facilitate mass meetings and action within several black communities in the South. For example, the growing use of telephones increased the speed of spreading messages; and the proximity of blacks to, and their concentration in, downtown areas facilitated the organization necessary for the success of the bus boycotts.[36] Important centers of activism were the black colleges, where students were recruited who had the time and motivation for mass protest. The indigenous roots of mass protest were the social conditions that had persisted in the South, and the movement gained strength as long as it concentrated its energies on the vindication of basic rights denied by local authorities.

The dilemmas within civil rights strategies were played out in internal organizational struggles. Internal struggles were intensified as the leaders of the movement attempted to relate their broadening political consciousness, which linked the activism that grew out of the South with worldwide racism and colonialism and radical ideologies associated with violent tactics, to the emerging racial unrest in the North and the antiestablishment mood of Vietnam War protests. The transition point for the movement was when the focus of protest changed from desegregation and voting rights to larger economic and political issues. At this point there was an ideological change in the spirit of radicalism, from a religious to a secular tone, that drew the more radical segments of the movement away from the moral outrage that gained its strength from the painful struggles in the rural South.[37] By the late 1960s, the movement's participants also realized that economic changes had not been stimulated by the most successful tactics of disruption, and questions were raised about whether civil rights tactics were appropriate means for challenging the economic and political structure of racial domination.[38] This disintegration was paralleled within the major civil rights organizations; for example, in SNCC the leadership crumbled as the group was subjected to external pressures and changing definitions of the movement in the early 1970s.

Retrospective evaluations of the spirit of activism have been conscious of the distinction between grass-roots rebellion and the push for equality through litigation. The mood at the time of the early protest activities has been described as the spirit of rebellion.[39] Excitement grew within the protest organizations as members sensed that they were part of a tide of anger so powerful that the white establishment was forced to respond. The protesters knew they were involved in a movement with historic proportions.

The mood of the movement at high tide, however, was different from the propensity for acquiescence that has permeated the everyday experience of oppressed people. The commonly held retrospective viewpoint on the civil rights society is that those who challenged the white establishment were inspired by the language of rights and that their fight was infused by the principle of equal treatment under law. Rosa Parks's dramatic refusal in Montgomery, Alabama, in 1955, to move out of the whites-only section of a bus is a symbol, for the civil rights society, of the power of rights-focused action. There is much disagreement about the intended meaning of her action, but it is fair to say that her refusal was not motivated by a narrow conception of legal entitlement but by her growing awareness of a group struggle and, more importantly, the simple fact that she could not "take it" any more. Yet, understanding Rosa Parks's action is more difficult than the conventional wisdom would have us believe—it shows that the expression of moral anger arises from violation of a person's dignity and may not be expressed simply in the language of rights. Rosa Parks acted with the confidence that she was not alone. Her actions were more than an expression of personal grievances; they were taken for the benefit of others.[40]

It is not my purpose here to address fully the factors that led to mass activism. In fact, I want to draw attention to the other side of the question, the acceptance of racial domination as it has continued to persist after the militancy of the civil rights movement. More directly, I hope to have evoked a contrast between the Reconstruction system of law, in which the black minority was the indirect (and possibly unlikely) beneficiary of laws that reaffirmed federal authority, and the period of civil rights activism, which was impelled by a ground swell of anger against the established hierarchy and its laws. As the role of litigation has become more central in the contemporary civil rights movement and grass-roots activism has declined, these two conflicting forms of action would lead us to question whether the legacy of race law may actually serve to cool the fires fueling the struggle against racial injustice.

The Historical Construction of Victims

The image of the victim of racial oppression, the slave, and later, the black citizen, arises from the social construction of the race problem. The characterization of the victims, by themselves and society, is created by a complex set of social processes discussed in the following chapter. The construction, however, should also be understood as a product of the historical transformation of race law and the identities of victims that were constructed, explicitly or implicitly, within legal discourse. How we see the victims of racial discrimination, and how much of their humanity we recognize, is thus preordained by the historical legacy that once classified blacks as nonpersons and later attempted to rectify this evil.

Corresponding to the moral decisiveness of the issue of slavery prior to the Civil War, the focal point of the rhetoric during that period was the issue of the *inhumanity* of the Southern way of life. Slavery was portrayed by the Northern abolitionists as a fundamental evil and by its Southern apologists as benevolent paternalism.[41] Beyond the rhetorical formulation, historical revisionists emphasize that slavery was a form of social control that evolved gradually and operated on a continuum of coercion. Slavery evolved into a "domestic" institution; thus, the legal position of slaves was determined by "political" slavery, "civil" slavery, plus "numerous calamities" resulting from "one man being 'subject to be directed by another in all his actions.' "[42] As the impediments of slavery reached into the domestic sphere, the humane treatment of slaves was increasingly guarded by their legal status. These changes in the legal status of slaves assigned new responsibilities to the master, but at the same time established the slave as a legal person, subjected to both protection and liabilities. These opposing tendencies created the following paradox, which Willie Lee Rose explains:

> [It allowed] abolitionists to assert that slavery was becoming harsher with each passing year, and enabled southern apologists to state, with equal confidence, that slavery was becoming milder. In fact, both sides were right, and both were wrong. As physical conditions improved, the slaves' essential humanity was being recognized. But new laws restricting chattels' movement and eliminating their education indicate blacks were categorized as a

special and different kind of humanity, as lesser humans in a dependency assumed to be perpetual.[43]

In fact, the new laws protecting the slaves consolidated the regime by creating "more regular and systematic labor." What was once achieved through force in harsher times was accomplished through a patriarchal diplomacy that avoided violence and created an illusion of "caring domesticity."

By the time of the era of constitutional reform beginning in the 1950s, there was a change in the rhetorical stance toward the situation of minorities. With the acceptance of the sociological approach taken in works like *An American Dilemma*, environmental constraints were seen as the barrier to the black minority's achieving equality. When these views were applied to the reinterpretation of antebellum master-slave relations, the issue of inhumanity no longer surfaced as the focus of the debate; instead, the fundamental inhumanity of the system was found to reside in social conditions.[44] Thus, historians assumed that blacks were "white persons" who had been subjected to abnormal and stultifying surroundings. The black person's reaction to the interplay of power relations, whether submissiveness or violence, was treated as a dysfunctional response. Both in the history of slave relations and in contemporary reform, negative qualities attributed to blacks were seen as failings that resulted as much from circumstances as from individual worth, and therefore should be sympathetically appraised. The moral guilt of the abolitionist was reborn in the consciousness of the contemporary reformer, and the guilt was appeased through the demonstrated generosity of the progressive thinker in accepting minority individuals of "lower merit" as equals. Yet Willie Lee Rose's characterization of the gradual acceptance of the victim's humanity can also be applied to the contemporary reformer. There is a paradox inherent in the contemporary system of reform: it gradually expanded its conception of the relevant social conditions that contribute to the black person's oppression, while at the same time granting these concessions based on blacks' classification as a disadvantaged group.

To the extent that systems of reform are gradual and the granting of civil rights depends on scrutiny of the social conditions rather than on reference to principle, the antidiscrimination strategy creates a "special and different kind of humanity" in the post–Civil War society. As long as the paternalism, explosiveness, and dependencies between white and black societies remain, the dynamics of the domesticization of slavery are recreated in the relationships between individuals who may formally possess equal rights, but where, in practice, one party suffers from the disabilities created by their low status.

The Proliferation of the Civil Rights Strategy

The analogy to Foucault's study of the discontinuities between pre-reform and Beccarian models of criminal justice is suggestive of the fallacies inherent in present strategies of civil rights reform. Current policies that justify a gradual process of reform are based on a faith in legal effectiveness that originated as part of a Reconstruction strategy of passive protection. Passive protection became the vehicle for courts to assume control over racial problems while at the same time disclaiming any responsibility actually to scrutinize the conditions of oppression. Antidiscrimination reforms continue to contribute to minimal progress because the measure of successful reform is the degree to which it protects the "special humanity" possessed by society's victims.

Despite the modest progress of the civil rights movement and the limited role of legal action in group activism, rights-focused strategies continue to be adopted by groups seeking reform. I have concentrated on the black civil rights movement rather than on other movements (e.g., the suffrage crusade) that parallel these struggles, because in some measure other groups model their approach on the strategies of legal protection. Organized groups are striving to achieve the same legal protection "won" for blacks to prohibit discrimination on the basis of sex, age, or sexual preference, and to control sexual harassment and pornography. Legal guarantees are secured as symbolic victories and as the initial step for powerless groups seeking improved social status. My reading of the history of the civil rights movement, however, raises concerns about the proliferation of civil rights strategies because it points out their limitations as tactics of liberation and demonstrates their origin in Reconstruction policies of social control.

Four / The Ideology of the Victim

When individuals claim that their unfavorable treatment stems from discriminatory practices, they assume the role of the victim. This transforms the conflict into an internal contest to reconcile a positive self-image with the image of oneself as a powerless and defeated victim. In this chapter I show that these struggles occur in a society where legal mechanisms, which create the victim role, maintain divisions between the powerful and the powerless by means that are obscure and hidden. The difficulties of maintaining individual or group identities in the context of complex and subtle social constraints are revealed in the following profiles of several respondents' experiences with discrimination.[1]

Carmen

Carmen considers her encounter with discriminatory treatment an inevitable event in the life of a woman of color. Carmen, who worked as a clerk in a discount department store for almost ten years, discovered that after a promotion to a more responsible position as an area supervisor, her salary was lower than those of men in the same position. Carmen chose not to make a formal complaint. She made this decision because of a complex set of constraints which reveal that her powerlessness in obtaining equal pay is linked to her powerlessness in other domains. She needs the job because she has responsibilities as a single parent of four children. She also recognizes that in any dispute it would be "me against a large corporation," and that then it becomes "your word against [a more powerful] somebody else's." There are risks in "not knowing what the outcome will be," and she has reason to suspect that the chances for successful resolution are low, having seen "too many people let go for things that make you wonder." Carmen justifies her acquiescence by explaining that she is like many people who, when something bad happens, "get it out of the way and don't make waves."

She avoids the full impact of accepting the definition of her problem as discrimination, and thus identifying herself as the victim, with careful distinctions about the nature of her mistreatment. Her employer may have discriminated against her "without even realizing it." Discrimination is ever-present; "you come across it so often it is really ridiculous." It is only when she hears certain insinuations that women are incompetent at their jobs that it gains conscious importance. Carmen attempts to avoid the label of victim by denying her group origins. While it is impossible for her to deny her womanhood, she can disavow her ethnic identity because of her coloring and married name. Therefore, she is not vulnerable to others who would say, "She is Puerto Rican, so we treat her *this* way." Discrimination is to Carmen something "they are constantly *pushing at you*." Avoiding acts of discrimination, given their ever-present nature, is impossible; what she dreads is the status of "being a victim of discrimination," a role that seizes and marks its possessor.

Despite her deliberate efforts to see her mistreatment as something other than discrimination, she confronts the reality of her circumstances: she was doing a good job and yet not receiving just rewards. For her to acknowledge an undeniable injustice, she must first come to believe that she has failed to live up to some preconceived standard of self-protection. She is burdened by her own estimation that she is "not that brave of a person." Confronting discrimination under these circumstances is a no-win situation that "depends upon you as an individual and how much you can take" (whether you are enduring precomplaint unjust treatment or postcomplaint retaliation). When Carmen feels depressed about what has happened to her, she has to remind herself that she "has nothing to be ashamed of."

Ironically, at the heart of the trap of victimhood is the strong and positive dimension of Carmen's self-evaluation of her experiences. Carmen prides herself on her ability to downplay the problem and act realistically. She is proud of her independence and her success in the personal domain of her family life. The pride in her own strength is linked to her identity as a woman. For example, in reference to her accomplishment of maintaining a house on her own for five years she proclaims, "I keep it going myself, I did it myself, a *woman*." She finds it necessary to remind herself that part of her identity, her womanhood, is capable of surviving. Thus, Carmen draws strength from her ability to endure, yet her energies are drained into the act of survival.

Carmen, in her acceptance of the role of the victim, avoids the sanctions that would follow from assuming the label of one who accuses others of discrimination, while submitting to the inevitable failure implied in her own standards of self-protection.

Helen

Helen has not gotten over the incident of age discrimination she experienced nearly two years before the interview. Everything happened all at once: her husband died, she was forced to adjust to living alone, she was mugged, and she lost her job. When she was then denied employment at a local department store on the basis of her age, Helen could not muster the strength to fight for the job. She describes herself as "not a fighter"; she chose to go home angry, rather than challenge the judgment of the head of personnel who told her that her age was the factor in the decision not to hire her. She felt that if she had gone back to the personnel officer and "told her a few things," she would have "put me down."

The incident provoked a mixture of two strong feelings. Helen has confidence in her abilities and feels that she has proven to herself and others that she knows "how to sell" because she was a competent salesperson of miniature furniture for more than twenty years. But, she also fears that she is "no good" to anyone any more. She had "gotten so old, it is like they should put me on a shelf and let me sit there." The incident of discrimination has become a harbinger of her ill-fated life in a society that degrades and isolates the elderly. She is fearful of the insults and injuries that will undermine her self-confidence and foresees a future filled with loneliness.

To appreciate why the incident of discrimination was so harmful to her sense of well-being requires an understanding of her dislike for impersonal situations. For Helen, all social actions involve either personal or impersonal treatment. She thrives when she receives personal treatment: from her former boss who gave her "freedom" and a "key to the building"; from the one of her three children who "understands" her; and from men whom she can "fix real quick." Impersonal treatment, however, is threatening and stifling. She felt like a "prisoner" at a former job where she had to punch a time clock. After a dispute with a police officer about crossing the street, she was offended and resentful of the authority of the police. Living in an apartment complex where she finds people unfriendly causes her to wonder if her neighbors "think I have horns or something." Although she recognizes that these instances of impersonal treatment threaten her sense of security, she feels helpless and embittered by their impeding presence in her life.

The incident of age discrimination Helen experienced was one more example of impersonal treatment. The dispute with the personnel officer began after she refused to put her age on the form. Helen claims age was not relevant, because she was "just what [they] wanted" for this part-time position. The head of personnel was the kind of person she "just didn't like" because she acted as if she was "better than everybody else" and as if "she knows everything." She expected that someone who was not so haughty would have been able to appreciate her experience and innate ability to sell. This type of employer would also have been able to recognize that Helen would put in "more than a day's work" in a congenial environment.

Her encounter with discriminatory treatment made her feel as if the impersonality of the social world had taken over her life. Why did others place so much importance on her age when she did not look or feel like she was seventy-six years old? Why wasn't it relevant to the employer's conception of "status" that through hard work she had surmounted the poverty of her childhood? Her financial security, therefore, no longer rests on her own labors but on Social Security, and all that is left is to "sit in my house all by myself." Her daughter tells her she lives in a "cave" because she is so frightened that she stays at home with the curtains closed. For Helen, the worst pain stems from being unable to understand the causes of her misfortunes. She identifies with the fate of her beautiful pet lovebirds: the birds died, even though she treated them well, fed them, and never let them out of their cage.

Delma

Delma saw the opportunity to be interviewed about her experiences with discrimination as a chance to purge herself of a gnawing sense of failure in her handling of the incidents and to possibly find a forum that would give some significance to her complaints. Delma recounted two examples of discrimination: one involved her dismissal from a car rental agency and the other was the outgrowth of bias against women in a current job requiring physical labor. In her first job she was demoted to "secretarial-type" work because the manager did not see "any advantages" in the advancement of women employees. She was infuriated when she was denied unemployment benefits owing to a misunderstanding about the conditions of her termination.

For Delma, sex discrimination creates confusion over "what it takes" to get ahead in society. She realizes that the privileged economic status of her family will not easily be achieved on her own, yet the hurdles appear ridiculously high. After she was fired from the car rental agency, she felt she had nowhere to go except possibly to work for her family as a strategy of last resort. She saw the lack of alternatives as "a sad comment on the employment structure."

Delma employs the concept of discrimination to account for the gap between her expectations of financial independence and economic reality. She sees herself as left in a state of limbo because she is not exceptional enough to bridge the gap. On one side of the gap is the image of herself as "a Jewish princess, [who gets] married and has babies." But the "problem is" that she does not "see that as an option." On the other side of the gap are the "fighters"—"women with a lot of experience in high-paying powerful jobs, and they get them because they fight for them."

Bridging the gap is difficult for all women because "nobody trusts you." Often your employer will wrongly assume that "you will get married and have kids," that "whoever you are sleeping with will support you," or that you are incompetent (and "their fear is that they will have to do my work and theirs"). The only reason why she and other women tolerate these situations is because they often do not have "any concept of what was happening."

Bridging the gap is difficult for Delma, partly because she lacks confidence. When she started a new career in the entertainment industry she was "terrified" ("I didn't know I could do it"). A more basic problem is her ambivalence over her desire to succeed. Her dilemma stems from the difficulty of forging a path where she feels comfortable both as a person and a woman. She sees her aunt as a model of success, yet her aunt is "totally against feminism and [at the same time] she worked all her life. She is a real advocate of getting married and being supported; it is ironical because she is the most independent woman I know." Her aunt is not her role model, however, because she cannot fit her own lifestyle into her aunt's idiosyncratic success story. Neither can she accept her aunt's complacency; "being treated like a woman" is too frustrating. Being approached in a discriminatory fashion is like "them saying they don't want you to contribute," and "they are playing with everything you have been taught. You are losing your femaleness, [which should not be] relevant as a professional." Her solution is consciously to protect herself from being "treated like a woman"—"I will specially cover any mention of sex, I will pay attention to my tone of voice, the way I am talking, the words I use, the way I approach someone." These tactics, however, only contribute to her impression that she is treated indifferently in the workplace.

Her overall reaction to her encounters with discrimination is that they have "changed my life totally." She believes she has no choice but to live with her frustration "until there is a larger percentage of women working," and then it "will be a lot easier." But, "I may never see it."

Laura

Laura reacted violently to an incident of discrimination, and after the confrontation she continued to be overcome by rage and confusion. By no means were her experiences with discrimination successfully resolved.

Laura was involved in two discriminatory situations, the first of which she labels as sex discrimination. A landlord "manipulated" her and retaliated when she "did not respond to his attentions." The dispute evolved into a battle over repairs in her apartment and ended in a city housing court hearing concerning rent withholding and damage to the property. The other incident arose after a fellow employee made a racial comment.

Laura believes she was "set up" to encounter discrimination on the job. She was "the only black woman there; I know I had been more or less hired as the token black there. [It was an] equal opportunity employer situation." As with the housing situation, in her job she was "manipulated to the point where I was put into this situation [of bitter confrontation]." She blames government for not doing things to "help her out" and for exposing her to the harms created by affirmative action: "I feel like maybe, if there wasn't so much wrapped into equal opportunity employer, then maybe I wouldn't have been in the situation."

Laura explains what happened after she asked a co-worker to retype a memo:

> She said that I was being shitty about this, that it didn't have to be retyped. And then she came back and said under her breath, "you black bitch." There was another employee sitting there that heard it, that made me take in that this had actually been said. . . . I went to her and questioned her about this, had she said this and she said yes that she had said it and I had heard her. . . . I went to the department manager and explained the situation. He said we were both in a state of pressure and that he was going to talk to her about it. I was in a pretty bad emotional state. I don't feel I should accept it under any circumstances. It just really, really got next to me. I went to him again, in about an hour. He had done nothing about it. At this time he told me to let him do his job and go and sit down. And that made me even angrier. He sat there talking to his wife on the phone. I went to this employee again; by this time I had completely lost my temper, and I told her if he is not going to do something about it I will and I slapped her.

When the commotion was over the manager sent Laura home on a three-day vacation. Laura was fired when she returned, in accordance with "company policy."

She did not fight her dismissal for two reasons. First, she felt she was partly in the wrong for her actions, although she strongly believed that the other employee should also have been fired. Second, each time she discussed the situation she would painfully relive it. The emotional consequences of the incident were severe and lasted for more than a year. Losing the job made her feel "like I lost an entire career. It took me a year or two to accept the situation. I will never forget it, I will never feel like I was justly treated."

In retrospect, she regrets both the violence of her actions and her inability to pursue her claim: "acting emotionally" accounts for both reactions. If these incidents happened today, she would seek legal counsel and take her rights to the "limit." Even though Laura claims to have become more assertive, her personal ideology reflects her reliance on "fate." She sees her disadvantaged position in society as the result of bad luck; she doesn't "feel like life owes me anything—all turns will be destined."

When concerns are raised about a victimized class, whether the causes are race, sex, crime, or other circumstances, the reality of victimhood is rarely seen as problematic. Victims are treated simply as members of a class or group that has been subjected to unfavorable life chances. To understand discrimination in American life, the status of victimhood needs to be seen as a product of the social imagination. To acquire the role of the victim is to have a particular type of power relations imposed upon one. Paradoxically, then, the social definition of discrimination has become a powerful tool for the creation of victims in contemporary society.

The Legal Forum and Victims

The word *victim* derives from the Greek *victima*, which means "a living creature sacrificed to a deity or offered in performance of a religious rite." Is the victim in contemporary society a victim in the Greek sense of the term? The idea of sacrifice, to choose a certain death and pass from the world of the living, cuts across modern and ancient meanings of victimization. Yet in the modern context, the conditions of the sacrifice change. In the classic use of the term, victims surrendered to tragic circumstances when they faced an inevitable choice between good and evil.

The legal forum of the trial has created its own great tragic victims. Otto Kirchheimer recounts the "two most momentous trials in history," the trials of Jesus and Socrates.[2] Both Jesus and Socrates in their political trials were able to represent a cause before the court and take advantage of the forum to publicize their purposes before posterity. Both Jesus and Socrates, in their defense, presented their cases so as to prevent any misinterpretation of their claims.[3] Jesus affirmed a spiritual claim before the court, his mission as the son of God, and defended himself from misinterpretation through silence. As for Socrates, he was to defend his system of free inquiry by reaffirming principle with an uncompromising defense and the sacrifice of his own life.[4] Jesus and Socrates made dramatic efforts to demonstrate the merits of their beliefs. Kirchheimer notes:

> [W]hat stands out in the cases of both Jesus and Socrates is the seemingly effortless consistency with which the trials merge into the total image of

what has come down to us as the essence of their historical personalities. . . .
Whatever their radically different foundations, religious experience or the
unceasing quest for enlarging the fundament of reason (and these differences affected their ways of arguing), both showed the same certainty in
defining and upholding their essential positions, which have left a lasting
impression on disciples and posterity alike.[5]

Through their trials, both Jesus and Socrates created historical per-
sonas. The tragedy inherent in their victimization was thus confined
to their personal sacrifices, because with their deaths their legacies
lived on.

Even though they were sacrificed, Jesus and Socrates were able to
use the legal forum to serve their political ends. As defendants, their
status as the accused was acknowledged by the structure of the trial.
Their mission was to design their defenses in such a manner that their
cases had impact beyond their personal fates. It is conspicuous that the
purposes of both trials were political; that the authorities had singled
out the defendants for prosecution because their ideologies and doctrines threatened the state. Like the tragic hero, they were engaged in
their own battles of good versus evil, and their sacrifice gained significance through identification with a transcendental cause.

For the modern victim of conditions, the victim of discrimination
cases, the judicial forum serves other objectives. For discrimination
cases there are no spectacular political trials.[6] The politics of the conflict have become more covert; the side of the victim and that of the
state have converged, so that the true victim of judicial authorities is no
longer the defendant in the case. The legacy of the trial is recorded in
the strategy of the prosecution and the doctrine of the judges, not the
words of the hero. The victim's historical personality is not relevant to
the discrimination case; it makes little difference who are the actors
involved.

The modern victims are sacrificed to their conditions. They are victims of economic class; they are victims of family structure; they are victims of extreme atrocities; they are victims of racial oppression. When
victims of conditions are convinced that their misfortunes are acts of
sacrifice, they are suffering from an illusion of choice. The illusion is
partly the creation of judicial institutions, in which the interests of the
victim are subsumed by the interests of the state. The tragic victims of
the political trial self-evidently are engaged in a struggle between a personal and historical identity and an oppressive legal power; they play
upon legal procedure to present a message to a sympathetic following.
Contemporary victims, however, are silenced by the role they would
play in the legal forum. Or they may be silenced because their message

is embedded in an unarticulated cause, which if stated would make their case self-evidently political. Instead, they pose the question, why is this happening to me? Their search for why they deserve their seemingly unfair treatment entangles them deeper in the psychological thickets of victimhood.[7]

The next part of this chapter describes how antidiscrimination law creates victims. Carmen's and the three other women's experiences serve as exemplary characterizations of discrimination victims. Most individuals who experience discrimination, like Carmen and the others, deal with the law indirectly, but this does not lessen the saliency of the legal realm to the transformation of their conflicts.

Identities in the Law

Legal authority is an intruding presence in everyday life. In Tocqueville's words: "It is a strange thing, the authority that is accorded to the intervention of the courts of justice by the general opinion of mankind! It clings even to the mere formalities of justice, and gives a bodily influence to the mere shadow of the law."[8] What is intriguing is not merely the reflection of justice found in the "shadow of the law" but how this reality imposes itself on a seemingly ordinary world. When law is seen as a social fiction, questions emerge about the relationship between the role performed and the audience. We discover, in subsequent chapters, that for the victim of discrimination the appropriate analogy for the presence of the law may be a genre in the manner of the theater of the absurd, where the law is a hostile and confusing force intervening in the personal sphere.

At the core of fictions created by the law are legal identities; the legal "person," "class," or "corporate" entity is construed in judicial arguments. The juridical person has a specified *visibility* and *presence*: the person is given an appearance in the image of the law.[9] The actions and interpretations of the legal conflict as described in appellate court opinions are, of course, far removed from the accounts of the individuals who are directly involved. The identities found in the law, moreover, constitute a powerful tool used to distinguish the interests of the person from those of the state. Legal identities are the social constructions that courts apply to recognize the role of the litigants. For example, the evolution of the concept of "standing" in public law links the juridical persons with their property interests. The term derives from the Latin *loci standi*, meaning "a place to stand," which evokes the geographical image of the individual and her or his property.[10] Standing is a device used in constitutional language to limit jurisdiction of official and public action, in fact, to remove private interests from judicial view.[11] The issue of standing means in practice that the person making a legal claim has suffered recognized legal harms and that the court is capable of providing remedies for those harms. The issue is raised when public and private boundaries become problematic (in some domains, the public nature of the contested issue is accepted, e.g., questions of fundamental constitutional rights; in other domains, the division between state and private interests is in dispute, e.g., environmental litigation). The interests of individuals are only considered in constitutional and administrative law proceedings when they fit into legal categories of "who" is harmed (class, group, etc.), and when their harm can be cast in terms of public values. By these means, private interests are selectively redefined as legal cases.

Legal identities shift the boundaries of the law; they are concepts that create tunnel vision in the law. Identities reinforce what Durkheim describes as the ephemeral distinctions between public and private law—all law is private in that it involves individual activity, and all law is public in that it involves social functions and roles.[12] Thus, legal concepts that identify persons before the law provide a fundamental way to create the public-private distinction, by making the primary issue for evaluation by the courts the individual's purpose before the law and the relevance of that individual's social role.

Cases of discrimination revolve around issues of identity. In the most obvious way, antidiscrimination law categorizes persons in terms of classes. The interpretations of the Fourteenth Amendment leave open the possibility of special protection, not only for former slaves, but for other "discrete and insular" minorities requiring special protection in the political process.[13] Many contested issues in discrimination cases are overt disputes over the classification of identities—criteria for suspect classification ("intent on its face" or "race-likeness" or judgments classifying perpetrators' actions in private or public roles).[14] In most instances, the expansion of the Fourteenth Amendment's guarantees hinges upon a redefinition of identities, both for persons suffering from discrimination and for the perpetrator.

Legal identities are symbolic representations. The law represents particular interpretations of reality or a retelling of a story about the incident and the parties involved. Whatever this reality, it is important that courts create perceptions that are acted upon.[15] When judges give content to the doctrines of "standing," "suspect class," or "harms," they define their own role as judges and they acknowledge identities for all those affected.[16]

The representation in law does not reflect any "whole" conception of the person. When individuals come before a court, they do not present themselves as they would in everyday life; instead, they come before the court in one of their roles.[17] In discrimination cases, the courts symbolically evoke a diminished role: the role of the victim.

Masks of the Victim

The fiction created by the law is a performance in which persons are represented by their "masks." The mask is a metaphor used to describe the construction of identities in legal reasoning. John Noonan's definition in *Persons and Masks of the Law* is "a legal construct suppressing the humanity of a participant in the process."[18] Noonan explains that masks of the law are not the private constructions of judges, but "socially fashioned" abstractions. Classifying human beings so their humanity is hidden is a form of alienation in legal reasoning. For the subject protected by antidiscrimination laws, the mask that hides her or his humanity is the mask of the victim.

The metaphor of the mask represents the concept of alienation. The image of the mask suggests that the true self is separated from an alien persona that is the product of legal reasoning. Alienation explains why most victims of discrimination appear to act passively and fail to pursue discrimination claims. Alienated persons feel no sense of interconnectedness as they play their social roles as employees, consumers, or citizens. There is no real sense of victory or defeat, no sense of responsibility, and no willingness to deal with frustration to strive beyond immediate satisfaction.[19] This stifles a sense of conflict; those who perceive discrimination do not extrapolate from their experience to a sense of social harm. They often fail to see their daily mistreatment as part of a larger struggle. And, perhaps more importantly, it enables those who experience discrimination to live with the division between an alien persona discriminated against in a social marketplace and a sense of inner self. The concept of alienation offers an explanation for why persons who experience discrimination are in a sense removed from their social conflicts, but the more intriguing implications of the image of the mask remain: the plot and the significance of the masquerade.

Victims of discrimination must struggle against their exclusion, not by asserting what they believe to be their true self-image, but by aspiring to the idealized victimization acknowledged within the law. Thus, the actual experience of alienation may not be a separation of selves but, rather, submission to a form of idolatry.[20] Idolatry takes place when people transfer their own life forces to things of their creation. Alienated persons become estranged from themselves, redeemed only by worship of and submission to their idols. Idolatry causes a sense of deadness and emptiness. In Erich Fromm's words, "The more man transfers his own powers to the idols, the poorer he himself becomes, and the more dependent on the idols, so they permit him to redeem a small part of what was originally his."[21] Idols drain people of their creative powers, leaving fewer energies to enrich their own potentialities.

To employ the concept of alienation does not necessarily suggest that the subjects of discrimination are wearing "false" masks. Consistent with the meaning of idolatry, people become estranged from themselves when they construct masks that are projections of victims and perpetrators in the law. Projection exercises an attraction for the victim because the law is seen as the ultimate means of vindication. As idolatry originates in religious worship of the gods, the legal system is worshiped as the paragon of freedom and equality. When persons see themselves in their legal identities, they are possessed by a false representation of the historical and social reality of progress against racial or sexual injustice. The creation of masks stifles the individual's ability to engage in conflict, but not only because there is a division between personal and social roles: more importantly, the legal conflict is suppressed because human energies are wasted on a reconstruction of legal masks created by judicial authorities. The purposes that this reconstruction serves are of paramount importance.

One woman who encountered discrimination in school, Sylvia, explained that without discrimination, "I would have thought more of me, myself." At times, she was comfortable with being labeled as Latin, but when enrolled as a new student in a school with a different ethnic composition, she found herself quickly categorized by the label "Mexican." She said, "Sometimes it would hurt, sometimes it would make me feel funny, *and well, I am Mexican*." Sylvia is expressing how someone in everyday life deals with masks of identity. There is a sense of discomfort, in that the all-inclusiveness of the label demeans her; at the same time, the label is deeply a part of both her social and her personal identity. To individuals who routinely encounter discrimination, the division between self and mask becomes a conscious issue in confrontations. They can often self-consciously distinguish the conceptions of the mask that represent qualities with which they identify from those conceptions that are imposed.

One of the most powerful depictions of masks of the oppressed is found in Frantz Fanon's *Black Skin, White Masks*. Fanon writes of the black person's identity: "At the risk of arousing the resentment of my colored brothers, I will say that the black man is not a man. There is a zone of non-being, an extraordinary sterile and arid region, an utterly naked declivity where an authentic upheaval can be born."[22] Fanon explains further that the black person does not rebel because she or he is enmeshed in the narcissism of the white person's mask. The member of the oppressed group becomes unable to extricate himself or herself from the alien image. Fanon speaks of the "sterile and arid region" in the black person's being, making it appear as if the oppressed have been invaded by a parasitic creature, a creature without a soul. To rid the self of the domination of masks is to discover there is an emptiness in part of one's constructed self-conception. One needs, however, not to discover a divided self, but to chase away a marauder.

Masks should not, however, be seen as totally alien from their wearer. Masks are the creation both of an individual and of powerful authorities. Studies of the way that people enact their roles show a range of levels of involvement, from total sincerity to total cynicism.[23] It is not, however, as if role-playing could be abandoned: it is essential to the ability to perform socially or to express oneself. As Sylvia reveals, in her discussion of her treatment as a Mexican-American, what seems alien is at the same moment essential to her being. With appreciation for persons' involvement with their masks, George Santayana observes, "Masks are arrested expressions and admirable echoes of feelings, at once faithful, discreet, and superlative. . . . I would not say that substance exists for the sake of appearance, or faces for the sake of masks, or passions for the sake of poetry or virtue."[24] Masks are no more human or inhuman than any other social expression, and they may reflect the interest of the wearer faithfully or unfaithfully. To move toward reclaiming the masks of victims, we need to understand the meanings created by these social constructions.

The Doctrine of Antidiscrimination Law

As discussed earlier, the basic logic of the antidiscrimination principle is to protect historically disadvantaged groups against identifiable perpetrators. A long series of court decisions have put remedial measures into action that are designed to make adjustments in the workings of the democratic process in order to serve the interests of these groups. Implicit in antidiscrimination doctrine are assumptions that create masks for the victim.

When judges fail to consider victims' potentialities and struggles, particularly in appellate decisions, their reasoning isolates the law from the victims' experiences. Instead, antidiscrimination law focuses on the perpetrator. Commenting on the perpetrator orientation of case law, Alan Freeman writes that the judges "see racial discrimination not as conditions, but as actions, or series of actions inflicted on the victim, by the perpetrator. The focus is more on what particular perpetrators have done or are doing to some victims than it is on the overall life situation of the victim class."[25] Given this focus, remedial action is aimed at the prohibition of illegal actions by a specific perpetrator and is narrowly fault-oriented. The role of the courts is to separate the few that discriminate from a "class of innocents."[26] This perspective, of course, assigns an active role to the court and to the cited offender(s) and constructs the victim of discrimination as passive.

The orientation of the law toward the perpetrator contributes to the invisibility of victims in legal reasoning. The need for stepped-up enforcement of civil rights is measured by the impact on the perpetrator —for example, the loss of job seniority for white males, the inconvenience of busing, and the extra training and recruitment costs for small businesses. The redistribution of resources among the "haves" is examined, not the consequences of the decision for the class of victims of discrimination. Ironically, the courts' careful evaluation of "just and humane" treatment refers to the negative consequences of antidiscrimination law on the class of perpetrators rather than on the victims.[27]

We can account for the logic of antidiscrimination enforcement by suggesting that victims of discrimination are categorized as political enemies. Speaking of the creation of political enemies, Murray Edelman observes that "intense animosities are aimed at classes of innocents" as an excuse for "accepting that ordinary beliefs rationalize punitiveness." Enemies are not ordinary antagonists: "Enemies...bear labels that highlight the covert, inhuman, incalculable qualities that make it impossible to deal with them as fellow human beings....it is *only* through names and other verbal signs that such nonvisible enemies are known and perceived. By definition they either act invisibly or their psychic malfunctions are internal."[28] Through language and categorization the enemy-victim is made invisible.

The image of invisibility gives unintended meaning to the well-known metaphor originating in Justice Harlan's dissent in *Plessy v. Ferguson*.[29] Justice Harlan's proclamation that the Constitution is color-blind foreshadowed the evolution of the antidiscrimination principle, which would adopt a state of blindness toward the interests of the victim. As Alan Freeman writes: "Color-blindness has become an abstraction that has taken on a life of its own, one that can turn around to disappoint the hopes of the very people on whose behalf it arose initially....It has become a way of abstracting the American black experience out of its own historical setting to the point where all ethics become fungible."[30] The courts are afflicted by a visual distortion of the individual's place within a historical situation. The most brilliant exposition of the meaning of invisibility from the perspective of the excluded is found in the prologue to Ralph Ellison's *Invisible Man*:

I am an invisible man. No, I am not a spook like those who haunted Edgar

Allan Poe; nor am I one of your Hollywood-movie ectoplasms. I am a man of substance, of flesh and bone, fiber and liquids—and I might even be said to possess a mind. I am invisible, understand, simply because people refuse to see me. Like the bodiless heads you see sometimes in circus sideshows, it is as though I have been surrounded by mirrors of hard, distorting glass. When they approach me they see only my surroundings, themselves, or figments of their imagination—indeed, everything and anything except me.[31]

If we understand legal authority to be one of the distorting mirrors, then we can see that its projection of the legal image of victims and their surroundings allows those in power to ignore the essential humanity of those who make claims of discrimination. The powerful effect of such invisibility is that it results in confusion over the effects of legal action on the intended beneficiaries. The presumption that the perpetrator is the targeted enemy of the state causes us to ignore the effects of antidiscrimination doctrine on the victim and to assume that the consequences of these policies are benign.

History and Stigma

The description of the persons who experience discrimination in case law is for the most part an empty characterization. The references are to the masks of persons whose situation is largely irrelevant to the reasoning in the decision. Imprinted on the masks is an image of discrimination, an interpretation of the individual's history and future and an impression of the harms that confront them.

How do the victims of discrimination wear their history in the writing of constitutional scholarship? They are often portrayed totally by their historical identity. The victim carries the legacy of slavery's "badges and incidents." Courts then play a remedial role by rectifying the wrongs inflicted upon similarly situated individuals in the past. Thus, it is the role of the court to rectify the historical record in order to make the victim *whole* again. The Supreme Court in *Franks v. Bowman Transportation Co.* (1975) announced: "We approved of a retroactive award of seniority to a class of Negro truckdrivers who had been the victims of discrimination—not just by society at large, but by the respondent in that case. While this relief imposed some burdens on other employees, it was necessary *to make [the victim] whole for injuries suffered* on account of unlawful employment discrimination."[32] The judges act as if they are reformulating the individual in the image of equality by reconstituting past and future and placing an artificial boundary on the relevant historical experiences of the wronged class. This logic also makes the right to a remedy historically contingent. The rationale applied in these decisions enhances the courts' abilities to limit or increase control over the perpetrators through the reinterpretation of history.[33]

For the class who experiences discrimination, their history becomes a burden, and the legacy of their mistreatment does not support their redemption but is used to betray them. The following passage by Frantz Fanon reveals how the linkage to a heritage of domination creates an invidious bondage with the past that prohibits the victim from influencing the future:

> Am I going to ask the contemporary white man to answer for the slaveships of the seventeenth century? Am I going to try by every possible means to cause Guilt to be born in minds? Moral anguish in the face of the massiveness of the past? I am a Negro, and tons of chains, storms of blows, rivers of expectoration flow from my shoulders. But I do not have the right to allow myself to bog down. I do not have the right to allow myself to be mired in what the past has determined. *I am not the slave of the Slavery that dehumanized my ancestors.*[34]

The doctrine of color blindness comes full circle in *Board of Regents of the University of California v. Bakke,*[35] where historical burdens and their consequences for the current status of minorities are considered irrelevant. In the *Bakke* case, the Court makes clear that in thirty years of interpreting the equal protection clause, the intent was "assuring to *all persons* equal protection of the laws" regardless of minority status or group history. And "because the landmark decisions in this area arose in response to the continued exclusion of Negroes from the mainstream of American society, they could be characterized as involving discrimination by the " 'majority' white race against the Negro minority. But they need not be read as depending upon that characterization for their results."[36] The Court ignores the history of past discrimination by assuming that the " 'majority' and 'minority' necessarily reflect temporary arrangements and political judgments."[37]

The expansion of antidiscrimination law beginning with *Brown v. Board of Education of Topeka* relied upon the recognition of the stigmatizing effects of social discrimination. The courts applied a "stigma theory," which maintained that the harms imposed on minority groups resulted from discriminatory legislative enactments (e.g., legally enforced segregation in the South). In the words of the *Brown* decision, "To separate them [black school children] from others of similar age and qualifications solely because of their race, generates a feeling of inferiority as to their status in the community that may affect their hearts and minds in a way unlikely ever to be undone."[38] For the Court to break down barriers established by precedent, it was necessary to justify the *Brown* decision with previously unrecognized "social facts." It is the stigmatizing effects of discriminatory state legislation, therefore, that justify the continuing role of the courts in regulating state action.

The stigma theory, however, distorts our understanding of the sources of harms imposed on racial and sexual groups. If the courts actually hoped to locate the social processes that stigmatize disadvantaged groups, they would attribute responsibility to factors that reach beyond legal enactments. Hannah Arendt has argued in her criticism of the enforcement of the Little Rock case (discussed in Chapter 1) that school desegregation decisions not only intervene in legal arrangements for school redistricting but impose the courts' authority upon inflexible preferences for "social exclusiveness" that are exercised in the private sphere.[39] Arendt sympathizes with the children and with the parents who refuse to submit their children to the pains of harassment, because the legal enforcement of desegregation policies unjustifiably violates their private choices. Her sympathy lies formally in a respect for private and public boundaries, but also reflects an understanding that stigmatizing effects, in this case, result less from legal regulations and more from deeply embedded social mores. The failure of the courts to recognize both private and public causes of stigmatization results in policies that place the burdens of social progress on the child. In other forms of discrimination, employment and housing, for example, victims suffer the burden of generally hostile working or living environments, while formal legal enforcement brings little or no relief for their problems.[40] Laura, for example, felt that equal opportunity laws had "set her up" for a chain of events beyond her control. Delma was acutely aware that she created a negative image of herself by playing either the traditional female role or the role of the woman who expects equal treatment.

The courts' stigma theory implicitly relies upon an unstated goal of assimilation and the assertion that law has the power to regulate the boundaries of group assimilation. The state's involvement in regulations that condone or encourage discriminatory practices is considered harmful because such regulations defeat "normal" processes of assimilation.[41] The long-term effect of the stigma theory the courts have applied is to create the illusion that victories for the excluded class have been won, while diverting attention from the social and personal oppression at the heart of the struggle by exaggerating the courts' ability to eradicate stigmatizing behavior.

Victims and Power Relations

Characterizing the problems and personalities of victims is a function of government agencies, courts, and professionals with jurisdiction over society's disadvantaged class of delinquents, welfare recipients, victims of crime, and the unemployed. These characterizations transform the lives of victims into cases, taking away from their stories the meaning behind their circumstances and unique identities. Michel Foucault describes the power of the biographical account in a disciplinary society:

> For a long time ordinary individuality...remained below the threshold of description. To be looked at, observed, described in detail, followed from day to day by an uninterrupted writing was a privilege. The chronicle of a man, the account of his life, his historiography, written as he lived out his life formed part of the rituals of his power. The disciplinary methods reversed this relation...and made of this description a means of control and a method of domination. *It is no longer a monument for future memory, but a document for possible use....*[T]he child, the patient, the madman, the prisoner, were to become...the object of individual descriptions and biographical accounts. *This turning of real lives into writing is no longer a procedure of heroization; it functions as a procedure of objectification and subjection.*[42]

The descriptions of the victims no longer take the form of tragic legends, nor are the actions of the victims "monuments for future memory." For the modern victim of circumstance the characterization of their lives will serve as a means to classify them into groups of powerless abnormals. The descriptions of victims' personalities (or their social psychology) individualizes their situation through a comparison with the norm. Individualization becomes a process of control—a mark of difference or a badge of stigma.[43] Foucault describes how this happens: "[W]hen one wishes to individualize the healthy, normal and law abiding adult, it is always by asking him how much of the child he has in him, what secret madness lies within him, what fundamental crime has he dreamt of committing."[44]

To liberate victims from their circumstances amounts to more than a new "heroization"; the richer portrayal of their lives in a literary sense cannot change their plight. But an important avenue to revealing the plight of the individual caught in modern conditions is an entirely different description of the victim—one that appreciates the power of the human spirit under extreme conditions of oppression. This account of victimization finds remarkable potential for the survival of human autonomy despite stultifying social conditions. The manifestations of victimhood can be recast as deliberate and narrowly constructive attempts to preserve identity. Thus victims, become engaged in a *politics of survival*—a battle designed to preserve the bare minimum of human autonomy.

The literature of social science unfortunately provides few accounts that revitalize the lives of victims. Perhaps the outstanding example is Robert Coles's series, *Children of Crisis*. Coles, in his accounts of the psychological effects of desegregation in Southern schools, found that black children showed extreme courage in response to threats and tormenting by white children and parents. One child's grandmother gave him the explanation that courage was the matter-of-fact result of having no alternatives—when danger is, as Coles put it, "everywhere, a never-ending consequence of . . . social and economic condition," then these dangers are expected and endured. Coles's reaction from interviewing black children throughout the South is that these children demonstrated "resilience" and "an incredible capacity for survival."[45]

An analytical exploration of the moral autonomy of the oppressed is found in the work of Barrington Moore, Jr. In *Injustice*, Moore examines the situations of ascetics, untouchables, and concentration camp prisoners because he considers them to have in common subjection to a universally perceived set of degrading circumstances, yet they accepted pain and submission with a degree of moral authority. As a result, each of these victims takes pride in their ability to endure injustices. Leaving the details of their self-repression for further discussion, Moore recognizes a capacity for moral courage—what he refers to as "iron in the soul." Iron in the soul is a capacity that some people have and others do not; it is a "capacity to resist powerful and frightening social pressures to obey oppressive or destructive rules or commands."[46] What appear to be acts of total submission may in fact preserve the remnants of human autonomy. The process of self-repression evolves into the destruction of self-esteem. People maintain a small sense of pride, however, by withstanding pain, avoiding confrontations, or completing humble work that fulfills innate desires for self-respect. Those who are denied socially defined measures of self-esteem are able to rely upon their most basic abilities. Individuals maintain their own dignity, despite the limited social world in which their dignity is respected.

The Manner of Victims

Individuals who believe that they have experienced discrimination will act in the manner of victims, reacting toward the actions of the powerful with characteristic language and manner of interaction. How do victims rationalize their powerlessness? How are these images of powerlessness created by both the victims and their adversaries? How are the images of the victim maintained and reinforced?

The word *victim* is used with hesitation, since the word evokes and reinforces its own social reality. The powerful and the powerless cannot be talked about in isolation from each other. The creation, maintenance, and destruction of the victim-oppressor relationship results from mutual exchanges. The image of the victim should therefore be seen as multidimensional, constructed by both the victim and those who impose their power.

We might question what is distinctive about victims. The perception of a powerless group as victims can be transformed if outsiders or group members focus attention on rectifying persistently unfavorable conditions, as, for example, when spokespersons for the urban poor organize a tenant's union, or members of the women's movement engage in consciousness raising. Thus, the social construction of victims is dependent on the stability of power relations; when activists challenge the definition of victims, they trigger counterreactions aimed at containing the potential conflict.

More specifically, there are three distinctive features of conflicts which create victims. First, these conflicts rely upon the docility of the oppressed. As Georg Simmel has theorized, extreme oppression leads to either extermination or enslavement. The strategy of conflict which contains victims, however, is a disguised and less extreme form of enslavement.[47] The retaliatory forces of the enslaved group are neither obliterated nor released; instead, the power relations fit the metaphor of being held below the boiling point, where a balance of overt and covert violence prevents the destruction of the relationship. Second, the creation of victims also depends upon a weak basis of group identity, where identification with others similarly situated does not lead toward the formation of bonds of strength but results in group weakness. Powerlessness is not possessed by the individual; it is a collective phenomenon.[48] For example, in some cases of extreme domination, the collective nature of victimhood is expressed in what Frantz Fanon describes as the native-settler "mass relationship." The effectiveness of brute colonial force is achieved by pitting native against native. The tension created by the settlers is channeled into "collective autodestruction," a death reflex that amounts to a communal form of suicide.[49] Collective consciousness works against the group by turning victims against one another. A third ingredient in the creation of victims is that they are powerless in a network of situations: home, education, workplace, politics. The interconnectedness of disadvantaged conditions often makes being a victim persistent and all-inclusive.

In the following section I identify several themes of powerlessness:

sacrifice, exclusion, and distortion.[50] The data are drawn from secondary sources of accounts of persons subjected to extreme conditions of victimization: slaves, victims of crime, women, and concentration camp prisoners.

Sacrifice

The noble connotation of victimhood is martyrdom. A martyr is able to win the sympathy of an audience and thus to share the burden with others. Victims who achieve martyrdom have not been sacrificed in vain but have offered themselves to a higher cause. Martyrdom is a means for a lone individual to act for posterity, fulfilling the ideal that, as Simmel says, the "personal is noble."[51] Therefore, the experience of victims is given its most honorable appearance by posing it as martyrdom, as with the use of the word *Holocaust*, meaning "burnt offering," suggestive of a noble sacrifice.

The worth of martyrdom derives from the will to choose to submit to a higher cause as well as identification with a group. Yet, modern victims fall short of this ideal of sacrifice; these victims both fear and envy their oppressors. As Herbert Marcuse suggests, the guilt feelings of the oppressed create a sociological dynamic whereby those who revolt identify with the powerful against whom they are rebelling.[52] It is this identification and guilt that creates the settler-native relationship previously described by Frantz Fanon: "Confronted with a world ruled by the settler, the native is always presumed guilty. But the native's guilt is never a guilt which he accepts; it is rather a kind of curse, a sort of sword of Damocles, for, in his innermost spirit, the native admits no accusation. . . . The native's muscles are always tensed. . . . The native is an oppressed person whose permanent dream is to become the persecutor."[53]

The victims are caught in a double bind of guilt, in which they are never totally convinced of their sin of transgression or of their innocence. Their identification with their masters evokes guilt about their own plight and the strength of their desires to transcend the situation. It also may serve as a means of preserving identity under extreme conditions. Eugene Genovese concludes that for American slaves, the "tendency [for] identification with [the] master reduced the possibilities for identification with each other as a class."[54] However, "slaves, by accepting a paternalistic ethos and legitimating class rule, developed their most powerful defense against the dehumanization implicit in slavery. Southern paternalism . . . unwittingly invited its victims to fashion their own interpretation of the social order it was intended to justify."[55] Because the paternalistic ethos implicitly accepted the slaves' humanity, it created a space for slaves to satisfy their own needs through religious expression.

The impression that guilt is the cause of sacrifice allows the actions of victims to be seen as willing submissiveness (passive victims marching to their death—e.g., the concentration camp prisoner) or as contentment and domesticated happiness (e.g., the happy homemaker). The image of willing submissiveness suggests that victims are content with their "punishments" and that victims suffer because of their own cooperation. In his classic 1948 study of criminal and victim, Hans von Hentig set up a scale of strengths of the "reciprocal operation of affinities between doer and sufferer," in which the victim is (1) apathetic, lethargic; (2) submitting, conniving, passively submitting; (3) cooperative, contributory; or (4) provocative, instigative, soliciting. For Hentig, these degrees of reciprocal affinities account for the "true nature" of the psychology of the victim-criminal relationship, which is not seen in the simplified vision of the law. In the law, "one is injured, the other is guilty. . . . It takes for granted that the doer is always, and during the whole process which ends in the criminal outcome, *active*, the sufferer always *inactive*."[56] The victim's role in provoking the doer is irrelevant in most criminal codes. In the interest of the victim, both the law and "reformers" put a double layer of guilt on the victim by attributing all action to the perpetrator. The ideology of criminal law renders victims passive agents forever caught in the inconsistency between the reality of their mistreatment and their denials that they "wanted it to happen to them." As with Genovese's observations of slave life, it is the slaves' identification with the master that provides the space in which they can create a social identity or a purpose for their actions.[57] The active role of the victims, thereby, goes unrecognized. Victims are caught in unresolvable guilt: either they desire to be like the oppressor and thus hold on to a wish to oppress the oppressor, or they want to justify their inaction and feel compelled to demonstrate that they played a passive role in their own oppression. When social critics defend the victim most vehemently, as in the victimology movement's defense of crime victims or liberal avowals of the industriousness of the unemployed, they intensify the sources of guilt and remove from view the active role of the victim. We are denied the opportunity to fully understand victims' emotional ties to their oppression in social constructions that rigidly defend them as innocents.

Exclusion

Victims are associated with covertly dangerous activities. They are often signifiers of what the dominant culture sees as evil; the extent of their evil may be criminality, deviance, nonconformity, or abnormality. The victim is identified as the source of others' hidden fears—as the unspoken cause of evil. When victims are created, social tensions are unleashed. The advent of the prosecution of witches, for example, corresponded with increasing political and social conflict; in colonial America, the clash between religious and civil authority marked the arousal of the fear of witches.[58] Witches provide an interesting example because with their labeling there is the invention of both criminal and victim in one. Witches play the dual role of victims of the sinister forces of the devil and of criminals, punished for their deviant behavior. Two devices of exclusion occur simultaneously. All victims to some degree fit the characterization of witches, being both possessed by evil and punished to contain the evil.

If the victims' actions are not intrinsically sinister, their violence or explosiveness sets them apart from the norm. Bruno Bettelheim's account of his own experience tells of explosive reactions among concentration camp prisoners. Bettelheim observed that being treated like a child by the guards created psychological reactions similar to those of children. It was difficult for prisoners to put their experiences in perspective. If they were pushed around by one guard, they reacted with extreme hatred toward the SS men, rather than focusing their anger on their internment. When they dreamed about revenge, it was over some minor incident, because, as Bettelheim suggests, the "extreme experience can not be dealt with through the usual mechanisms of anger and revenge."[59] The pressure of domination creates strain and tension that may allow only for explosive reactions and counterreactions. Genovese describes the slave-master relationship as caught between severe cruelty and submission. Any challenge to the authority of the master was a threat to both slave and family relationships, so any act of disobedience "had dangerous consequences."[60] The potential of explosion reinforces inviolable bonds for victim and oppressor. There are no minor infractions within "normal" ranges of behavior; there is only rebellion or submission.

Distortion

The ideology of the victim rests upon a view of the world that separates psychology from politics. From this viewpoint, the irrationalities within society are commonly seen as individuals' irrational behavior. Consequently, we fail to appreciate that what may appear to be a strategy to avoid, hide from, or submit to social pressure may be evidence of a victim's will to survive. The problem with the criterion of rationality is not only that it reinforces the social standards of the powerful, but that it assumes that the victim has the same needs as those who are beyond fear and want. In extreme conditions, the definition of rationality changes.

The image of the split personality is often imposed on classes of victims. Susan Griffin sees the theme of separation as a theme of womanhood: the separation of anger from her body, the will from her head, the knower from the known. Griffin parrots the message of male society to women: "They said that in order to discover truth, they must find ways to separate feeling from thought. . . .emotions they said must be distrusted *because we are filled with rage* that where emotions color thought *because we cry out* thought is no longer objective *because we are shaking* and therefore no longer describes what is real. . .*because we are shaking in our rage and we are no longer reasonable.*" [61] Reason, as interpreted by a male society, requires the separation of emotion from thought. It is claimed that victims are unable to confront pain, hurt, emotions, as an integrated vision because the intensity of feeling may lessen their ability to deal with the situation in a "rationalized" world. The ability to make this separation that women and other victims are "incapable" of achieving is seen as integral to all rationalized thinking.

Victims are characterized at two extremes: either their hysterical reactions prevent clear-sighted thinking, or a total breakdown between reason and emotion produces a split personality. The separation of the subject from the object, reason from emotion, or the real from the unreal is not a "problem" experienced by victims encountering a situation; it is a powerful mechanism for survival. Bettelheim explains that he survived the concentration camp because he was able to detach himself from degrading experiences by separating what was happening to "him," as a human, from things happening to "him" as an object. Other prisoners put this same feeling in more general terms, claiming that the "main problem is to remain alive and unchanged."[62] Through detachment they were able to maintain the integrity of their personalities. When victimization becomes an integral part of a culture, this "irrationality" takes the form of rituals. Genovese writes that the madness of slaves' ritual was part of their salvation: "the slaves' wildest emotionalism, even when it passed into actual possession, formed a part of collective behavior, which the slaves themselves controlled." The religious ceremony, which to the observer demonstrated the slaves' loss of control, was a means of containing emotionalism. "[E]cstasy [found in rituals] may become an instrument of salvation or self-deification."[63] Thus, behavior that observers may describe as collapsing in response to social strain is a means of preserving identity; it ensures survival when one is faced with an abusive reality.

Another impression of victims' distortion of reality is the claim that they lack a sense of realism. They are criticized for living in a fantasy world. Although the conditions of their victimization may justify a sense of hopelessness, derogatory references are often made about their acceptance of fate. Elizabeth Janeway reasons that "fate" has a female gender because "[f]ate represents the rejection of the plans of the powerful by the weak. To see the embodiment of this rejection as female points...to the central position among the weak which is held by women, who have been traditionally the creatures furthest removed from the ability to act effectively in the external world."[64] Those who accept their fate are in a double bind; their submission destroys reasoned plans and ambitions yet they cannot control the negative consequences of their acts. The image is used in contemporary politics to describe the plight of the poor and disadvantaged: on the one hand, their problems persist because they are resigned to their fate; on the other hand, they are at fault for their unacceptable behavior that destroys peace and order.

In the fantasy world of the victim, there are imaginary boundaries between the powerful and the weak. Abused children coming to grips with more favorable conditions of dependence confront what has been described as the fear of "slaying the dragon." "This dependence gives our ideas of power a built-in ambiguity. . . . if we push too hard . . . if we try to behave as king of the universe. . .we in effect destroy these others as companions and peers to whom we can look for help in difficulty."[65] Richard Sennett, speaking of the false love for an authority figure such as a paternalistic employer—in this case, the Pullman Company— reveals how fantasies create ambivalence toward authority, because we fear that pushing too hard will force those whom we rely upon for security to abandon us.[66]

These themes reveal how the distortion of victims' social reality to themselves and others is a barrier to their liberation. The limited imagination of the victim may be a more powerful deterrent than social and economic resources. The "psychology" and "politics" of victimhood prohibit an exercise of their full human powers. Their exercise of power is unable to capitalize upon personal strengths: given a series of dichotomies (private-public, immoral-moral, weak-powerful, objectified-humanized, irrational-rational), the victim is pushed to the side of weakness and vulnerability. The exercise of power for victims is therefore not perceived as political, or it is trapped in ambivalence: power for a private cause is martyrdom, power for immoral reasons is criminal, power for unrealistic causes is irrational.

The analysis of victims in their social context suggests two ways of viewing their struggles: thinking about their psychology as a political expression and reintegrating the victim-oppressor perspective. Undeniably, victims possess a social psychology of their own. Examples given here rely upon its distinctive characteristics, but the interpretation of victims cannot be revolutionized without a new understanding of their psychological characteristics. Victims do not possess intrinsic psychological aberrations; they are a part of an interchange of power which elicits these reactions. These distinctive behaviors can be seen as more than psychological, meaning that they cannot be interpreted within a conventional definition of rationality. An entirely new focus on victims' struggles is developed here in terms of the "politics of survival."

Reintegration of the victim-oppressor relationship is taken literally by Bruno Bettelheim. Bettelheim believes that to recover from victimization requires a process of reintegration—doing something with and about the experience. This often involves recognizing the small part the victim played in encouraging the abuse.[67] The recommendation for reintegration, translated into theory, implies that victims need to be seen as active participants in the formation of the victim-oppressor consciousness. The psychology and politics of victims and oppressors have much in common. Hannah Arendt's description of Eichmann as the archetypal villain arising from the tragedy of modern conditions brings forth the psychological features of banality, loss of meaningful expression, double-edged guilt, and a personality attempting to survive in an amoral world.[68] The similarities and differences between villains and victims are striking and illustrative of the web of distorted uses of power within which the two sides are caught.

Five / The Ethic of Survival

The last chapter described the invisible bonds of victimhood. This chapter will put these themes of victimhood in the context of individual encounters with discriminatory practices. Individuals fail to struggle against discrimination when they accept the invisible bonds of victimhood: exclusion, sacrifice, and distortion. The most obvious barriers to initiating a claim of discrimination are structural constraints (e.g., lack of resources for legal assistance, unemployment insurance regulations, or administrative record keeping).[1] While these are serious deterrents to pursuing claims,[2] to focus on them is to make a basic error. Such an exclusive focus suggests that, absent such barriers, victims have absolute freedom of action and that if the barriers were removed, they would be able to expend their full energies on the attainment of their legal rights. This exploration of the internalization of power in discrimination conflicts reveals there are more subtle barriers to legal action.

The Creation of Illegitimate Bonds

Discrimination conflicts usually occur in situations where there are asymmetrical power relations.[3] In most instances of discrimination the perpetrator acts in an authoritative role (employer, landlord, or teacher, for example). In these roles people wield power by virtue of their expertise, their ability to enforce orders, the permanence of their positions, or their mystique. The perpetrator's advantage can be as overt as the victim's recognition that persevering in a complaint is at the cost of submitting to arbitrary power, or as subtle as the victim's internalizing the authority's negative image of her or his group.

The attitudes toward authority of those who experience discrimination stem from the prevalent assumption in democratic societies that authority is benevolent.[4] A paternalistic vision of the state creates a pattern of docility that emerges in indirect relationships between the state and individuals, such as in relationships with employers and government officials. The individual is lulled into an acceptance of dependency that inhibits resistance to discriminatory practices.[5]

In fact, when discrimination disputes occur, the ordinary assumptions about the legitimacy of an employer's or other authority figure's actions dissolve as people recognize that they have been singled out for adverse treatment. A more volatile and destructive form of control evolves as the victim attempts to make sense of one person's arbitrary imposition of her or his prejudices and the legitimacy of her or his actions by virtue of occupying a certain position within a powerful institution.

The participants in this study who experienced discrimination often portrayed perpetrators as tyrants. Several individuals referred to the "regal" qualities of those who discriminated against them. Helen, when denied a job in a department store, reacted toward her employer in these words: "She is very attractive. She'd wear clothes like she stepped out of a spring garden. She'd walk like a model; she was something else. You'd have to see her. She had an office in the back of the store. She sits like she's the *Queen*, Queen Elizabeth. Like you'd have to *bow down to her*. That's the feeling I get when I see her." Helen was intimidated by the personnel officer's regal appearance. She was particularly sensitive to the way in which the environment surrounding the woman was designed to impress her "subjects" and protect her authority. She was, in fact, afraid to begin a disagreement because she felt she lacked the language skills and the social presence to confront her opponent.

Carmen also described her supervisor on the job in regal terms: "He was a bit of a *tyrant*—screamed a lot and yelled a lot. The type of person who would make you cry, then apologize instantly. Like, heck, I am the boss and the *ruler*, and I do things my way, always." Carmen considered her employer's demand for total control immature, like the actions of a brutal ruler. Even though she responded more cynically to the regal manner than did Helen, she felt caught in an explosive and abusive exchange.

Other tyrantlike employers achieved total control through verbal abuse. Nora believes that she never received an explanation for her pay differential because "to be quite honest with you, [we] were terrified with the owner of the company. He ran a very tight ship, and if you disagreed with him you were sure to cause nothing but trouble." The tactic of a less effective tyrant (a military dictator), Virginia's supervisor, was to impose a chain of command that allowed the top ranks to reserve credit for accomplishments. To Virginia he was the "chicken colonel" (he was a former army colonel) because he could exercise authority only behind closed doors (but paper-thin walls); Virginia was his "secretary," and so he claimed credit for her work.

The rulers may also be patriarchs who have lost their honorable airs. John explains that his district supervisor "did not really talk, she picked at me. She talked at me. Like ah, say parents do their children. That is how she handled me, in fact she called me her *problem child*. I had a few names for her." The childish treatment is resented, but at the same time it stifles all communication and provokes a simple response. Sometimes the tyrant can appear to others as respectable and wise. Delma describes her employer as a man who was "terribly kind, generous, cute, good looking—the darling of the company." She felt he was doing what was best for the company, despite the fact that it meant that she was considered insignificant in relation to the greater good of the company and that his behavior toward her was "cold and cruel."

The authority figures described by these participants behave according to Machiavelli's instructions to the prince: they control by fear and simplification of reality.[6] As tyrants the perpetrators are brutal simplifiers of the situation through appearances that disguise realities. The effectiveness of their rule, according to Machiavelli, rests upon the subject's willingness to be "always taken by what a thing seems to be and by what comes of it."[7] The employee believes "what seems to be"—that his or her supervisor exercises royal supremacy and "what comes of it"— the finality of the authority's total control. All conflicting interests and demands are subdued by the employee's fearful withdrawal. The bonds of the tyrant image are powerful because the disrespect for royalty is self-deceptive; it allows the subjects to regard their superiors as immature and arrogant and yet justifies their own impotence. Tyrants are not legitimate rulers; yet for individuals caught within these demoralizing conditions the illegitimacy of the rulers sustains rather than defeats them. The image of the tyrant transforms the exchange between perpetrator and victim into a situation in which the perpetrator controls and the victim transgresses.

The invisible bonds of victimhood are also maintained by the confused reactions of these individuals subjected to discriminatory practices. The confusion is immobilizing because the victim is thrown into a futile search for satisfactory explanations. A Chicana who worked in the personnel department of a large corporation was bewildered about her lack of opportunity for advancement. Although she recognized that she and two black women were not receiving the same treatment as others, she was puzzled: "I would not get the chance. Not me. And I would wonder, why not me?" As a black person in an employment dispute simply states: "I couldn't understand why they were doing this to me. Well, I *understood why*, but. . .why did they hire me in the beginning?" Delma also describes her disorientation: "It took me six months to a year to realize people are like that. . .that nice people do that sort of thing."

Discriminatory treatment may transform ordinary situations into brutal events that are hard to comprehend. A young Mexican-American woman abused by other students in a predominantly black high school expressed bewilderment about the absence of basic human respect: "I was thinking to myself this couldn't be possible, how is this happening? How could kids, human beings, be like this?"

Confusion in discriminatory situations is often the consequence of ambiguities about racial boundaries. People of color may think they have learned the rules delineating the peripheries of acceptability, only to discover that what provokes discriminatory retaliation is found out solely through experience. Patricia's reaction to discrimination is often "not hostile as much as *puzzled*." She explains, from a historical frame of reference, that prior to the 1960s a black person was "emotionally more stable" because there were known "clear-cut limits." As a child, she recalls, "being black was easy"; for example, one knew not to trespass on the neighboring white community. As the civil rights movement progressed, however, the lines became "invisible"—like a "smoke screen" that is there "but kind of fades." She feels that the invisibility of the lines today ("you have to fall on them to know about them") creates confusion more painful than the insult of the blatant denial of privileges in the past. A woman who experienced sex discrimination was unable to describe (or perhaps justify to others) her reactions to ambiguous boundaries: "it is like someone physically moving in on your territory. There is a line. I don't know how to explain it. It made me feel a little bit angry and helpless."

The victim's sense of confusion often determines how the conflict unfolds. At important junctures in the conflict, the victim is led into feelings of uncertainty and powerlessness. For example, when Deborah persisted in asking why she was not hired in a caretaker's position in a home for the handicapped, the employer finally said "it was because I was not a man, and I said I can't get a sex change operation, can I?...I just felt real powerless." Perplexed individuals see a series of events over which they have no control as self-perpetuated and continue to question whether their actions will threaten an already unfortunate state of affairs.

The potential for explosion reinforces the inviolable bonds of the victim-oppressor relationship. Since the expression of anger is unacceptable in bureaucratic settings, there are no minor infractions within normal ranges of behavior: there is only rebellion and submission. The victims of discrimination, therefore, perceive their own reactions to injustice as explosive and extreme. Most of the individuals admitted to extreme anger (often violent in intent) that persisted for long periods of time. Helen, who was in her seventies at the time she was involved in an age discrimination dispute, said in reference to her employer: "I wanted to punch her. I was angry for a couple of weeks. I would like to take a good swing at her and teach her a couple of things....I'd still [two years later] like to punch her." Another woman, after being fired, claimed, "I felt like bombing the place." John indicated that he was so angry that he could not deal with it verbally; if he expressed his rage, he would have to "take it out on the street." Carol, in a sexual harassment dispute with a fellow employee, felt, "There are times I would love to punch him out—to get out the frustration." Patricia, after being fired from a newly acquired job because they were "looking for a white person" to fill the position, was angry for months. Two to three years afterward it would make her angry whenever she thought about it. In only one case in the study did anger lead to physical violence: Laura had slapped a white, fellow employee who had made a racist comment.

These people seemed to respond to the violation of their dignity within these power relations with intense anger, expressed in the very terms that had been prohibited—immediate physical retaliation—but the result was that anger silenced the victims. They were intimidated by the social unacceptability of their anger; therefore, they confronted their emotions by exercising control. As Patricia explains, she can only remain angry if it is "vital"; otherwise, if she let herself get angry, "then I'd be angry all the time." Others admit they "don't know how to fight," "stay quiet," "calm down," or "absorb a lot of anger before [they] let go." These rationalizations about the desirability of control may stifle the expression of injustice in any form.

Most of the individuals interviewed, to greater or lesser degrees, also perceived the endurance of mistreatment as a form of sacrifice to unavoidable misfortune. The ethic of sacrifice arises from their acceptance of an implicit theory about the cause of prejudice in society. This notion of prejudice attributes the perpetrators' actions to personality flaws. These people are "immature," "just plain ignorant," "unable to deal with frustration," or act unjustly because they are "petty and stupid." Thus, in the mind of the victim prejudicial actions are isolated from causes and consequences. They simply anticipate that in democratic societies some "intolerant" personalities are prone to prejudice owing to their unresolved psychological anxieties, cultural isolation, or punitive nature.

The ideal of sacrifice enables these individuals to believe that by responding passively they demonstrate their own strength of character. They may even believe that their fate is indistinguishable from others', regardless of issues of race or sex: everybody encounters the infrequent perpetrator of malicious behavior, some of whom employ negative stereotypes.

This theory, which identifies prejudice with individual intolerance, is advanced by Gordon Allport in *The Nature of Prejudice* as consistent with the American ideal of progress: Americans have a great faith that attitudes can be modified; even though this faith may not be entirely justified, the fact that it exists may make change come about. Allport argues that viewing prejudice as caused primarily by social structural factors is too pessimistic—that change in a system "must begin somewhere," and the psychological system may be in an unstable equilibrium most susceptible to positive intervention through education or publicized moral approbation.[8] The difficulties inherent in this notion of attitude change become evident when one attempts to apply it in social interactions.

By holding on to the belief that prejudice is rooted in individual psychology, victims contribute to the effectiveness of discriminatory practices. First, they are unable to view perpetrators as enemies and to channel their hostilities. For example, one woman seemed unwilling to make the connection between people who "act out frustrations" and express irrational "dislikes" for Mexican-Americans and the systematic bias she found in media reporting of immigration problems that singles out Mexican nationals from other foreigners. The connections are not salient because her encounters are not with her "enemies." The type of confrontation that would promote attitude change or discourage the actions of intolerant individuals is avoided.[9] When victims choose to see each incident as an isolated occurrence of prejudicial treatment, or when they avoid face-to-face confrontation, they lose the opportunity to exercise their power.

Consider two confrontations that were never realized. Patricia, when she returned to pick up her final check from her employer, found the woman "embarrassed," like "someone who made a decision they are not proud of." Patricia recognized that if she started a confrontation, the employer "would get very upset." This confirmed Patricia's suspicions about the discriminatory nature of her firing. John describes a similar incident with his district supervisor: "All of a sudden he gets loud and tells me he is not prejudiced. I didn't ask for that, I just looked at him, walked out, and I let it go at that. . . .That is the main incident that let me know what was happening, that let the cat out of the bag."

When the perpetrators acted as if they were embarrassed, John and Patricia were, to a small degree, vindicated by their employers' subtle admissions of guilt. But John and Patricia did not initiate the confrontation that would elevate the sense of embarrassment to a forced defense of prejudicial treatment. Instead, they permitted discrimination to be practiced in covert and indirect ways (and chose not to learn more about the motivations behind their employers' actions) by sacrificing themselves to random acts of prejudice.[10]

The promise of antidiscrimination law is that it will benefit the victim against the more powerful perpetrator of discrimination. These struggles usually end in defeat, however, because the bonds of victimhood inhibit challenges against the perpetrators. The result is that victims internalize the power struggle by submitting to ruthlessness and their own anger and confusion. The adoption of an ethic of survival justifies as heroic their choice to submit to their powerlessness.

Assimilation and Exclusion

Beyond each incident of discrimination, those who are subjected to hostile treatment, on the basis of their identifiability as members of racial, sexual, religious, and other groups, encounter a lifetime struggle to preserve their identity. Before describing how the participants in this study respond by adopting an ethic of survival, I begin by drawing portraits from two biographical accounts that capture the extreme effects of social discrimination on the personality. These accounts describe how the response to the assault on identity instigated by acts of discrimination is influenced by the ideologies of assimilation and exclusion. The impact of the forces of assimilation is found in Hannah Arendt's analysis of the life of Rahel Varnhagen. The personality driven to strategies of exclusion is seen in the life of Malcolm X, as he described it.

Rahel Varnhagen

Rahel Varnhagen (1771–1833) was a Jew caught in the dilemmas of a period of assimilation in Germany. She lived during a time when "the gates of the ghetto" were open and Jews in Berlin sought escape from German Jewish society. Rahel's life was a struggle to separate herself from her history. In her dying words she expressed these regrets: "With real rapture I think of these origins of mine and this whole nexus of destiny, through which the oldest memories of the human race stand side by side with the latest developments. . . .The thing which all my life seemed to me the greatest shame, which was the misery and misfortune of my life—having been born a Jewess—this I should on no account now wished to have missed."[11] All personalities are the product of an individual history and the culmination of their heritage. Arendt observes that freedom from history comes only with its direct confrontation: "Whoever wants aid and protection from History, in which our insignificant birth is almost lost, must be able to know and understand it."[12] In Rahel's situation, to know and understand history would require an acceptance of the Enlightenment vision of progress through assimilation. The Jewish culture of which Rahel found herself a part strove to separate her from history. The attainment of wealth and the gentrification of the Jewish culture was the means of escaping the ghetto and beginning the process of assimilation.

Rahel's was a personal struggle, in which she failed without excep-

tional gifts—she was "[n]ot rich, not cultivated, and not beautiful—
that meant she was entirely without weapons with which to begin the
great struggle for recognition in society."[13] She did achieve, by establishing a salon that served as a meeting place for figures in the Romantic
movement, a small place for herself in society and thus a place in cultural history. Arendt, assessing the mood of the period, notes that "[a]
political struggle for equal rights might have taken the place of the personal struggle. . . . Jews did not even want to be emancipated as a whole;
all they wanted was to escape from Jewishness, as individuals if possible. Their urge was secretly and silently to settle what seemed to them
a personal problem, a personal misfortune."[14] Arendt associates the
attitude toward assimilation with the Enlightenment belief in progress.
The reform of society would not evolve through personal struggle but
by bringing into the "fold of humanity" those who are oppressed.[15] To
assure the rights of all people required that rights be granted to Jews;
"[t]he cause of humanity thus became the cause of the Jews."[16]

Rahel was involved in a personal struggle in a larger sense, in that
she took refuge in herself for protection. She rationalized through the
denial of her mistreated identity. At age twenty she wrote, "I shall never
be convinced that I am a Schlemihl and a Jewess; since in all these years
and after so much thinking about it, it has not dawned upon me, I shall
never really grasp it. That is why 'the clang of the murderous axe does
not nibble at my root'; that is why I am still living."[17] Engaged in "acts
of self thinking," Rahel created a "sphere of pure ideas" that could escape the blows of fate. Convinced of inevitable evil in the outside
world, "there is no reason to feel shock at having been struck this one
particular time." These virtues of the Enlightenment, reason and
introspection, preserve the "power and autonomy of the soul. . . . at the
price of truth . . . for without reality shared with other human beings,
truth loses all meaning."[18] Not only did she seek insulation from the
reality of her Jewishness in a state of mind, the course of her life was a
series of flights from despair—through intellectual and cultural en-
tourages, through romantic love, and finally through a "titled" marriage and a new name.[19]

Her struggle evolved into a confrontation with her own illusions.
Her new name taken after her marriage "was intended to help her
become one human being among others." Arendt explains that it is as
if Rahel believed she could cover up the nakedness of her Jewishness.
She was "[f]ull of illusions about the possibilities of the outer world, she
imagined that disguises, camouflage, changes of name could exert a
tremendous transforming power."[20]

Arendt identifies Rahel's ultimate paradox as the desire to prove
oneself an exception (given the undeniable existence of a historically

excluded group of Jews) as a means of being declared "normal." Her life was a never-ending appeal to others for recognition that "I am not like them"; an appeal that was never heard.[21]

Malcolm X

The Autobiography of Malcolm X is an American classic because this rebel's experiences are an indictment of American society. The story of Malcolm X is an account of a man who survives through his exclusion. The young Malcolm grew to adulthood even though racists killed his father, his family was split apart by welfare bureaucrats, he was forced into poverty or into taking charity, and all his aspirations were discouraged.[22] He was engaged in a battle between individual and institutions; each of the latter (welfare, school, foster home) had its own idea about who Malcolm should be.[23] Those who were most benevolent, like his last foster parents, were most destructive of his self-esteem.

His response was retaliation through a strategy of "power at the extremes." He was able to realize how little he had to lose in his state of socially created inhumanity; he used irrationality to strike out against society. He retaliated with violence. When carrying weapons, he could kill or be killed at any moment. He forced the peacekeepers constantly to monitor him. Malcolm X made himself visible; with flamboyant dress, he could announce to society that he was neither assimilated nor defeated. He was flaunting his unwillingness to fit into the stereotyped image of the passive black.[24]

His power, attained through exclusion, only allowed him to prey on the weak—it was self-deceptive. As a drug pusher, he sided with the powerful economic organization that fed drugs to the ghetto; as leader of an organized theft ring, he preyed on the rich by letting them set themselves up through their own weakness and greed. As a criminal he satisfied his hunger for power, but it did not reach to those who dominated and oppressed him.

Malcolm X was a person made stateless by his race. He was disowned by the institutions that provide order, rights, and protection. Left to defend himself, Malcolm was drawn to the Black Muslim movement because it gave him the security he could not find in the dominant society. He was able to identify with a creed in which race and religion were united in a worldwide struggle. It gave Malcolm X a sense of pride in his racial identity, a reason for living in America and not being a part of the white culture. He reclaimed his history through identification with the Black Muslim struggle and a future directed to the building of a new nation, the Nation of Islam. A new sense of humanity was realized when he had reason to trust other people who were devoted to the same cause and when he gained a family of new "sisters and brothers" and brought together his family of origin.[25]

A potent symbol of the Muslim identity is acquiring X as part of one's name. X is a substitution for the slave name, and thus "the 'X' symbolizes paradise lost, with the reminder that the devil is responsible for the loss. It also embodies the idea that its bearer is an *ex*-slave, an *ex*-Negro; that is, he acknowledges his past slavery, and thereby entitles himself to a justified hatred of the slave master."[26] The Muslim recreates himself, in a powerful rather than a submissive image, through the new name.

Even though Malcolm X found security and fulfillment of other basic needs in the exclusive ideal of the Black Muslim revolution, he did not find his individuality or his free will. Independent thinking was inhibited by the insistence on total acceptance of the prophet's interpretation of the principles of the Muslim religion. He was an adherent and then leader of a movement that was held together by a concentration of power in tyrannical and charismatic authority.

For Malcolm X, the strategy of exclusion was transformed within a lifetime into a flight from the reality of politics. The Black Muslim group was cornered and driven into radicalizing its means, particularly toward violence and counterracism. Its strategies were ultimately counterproductive, given the limited resources of its followers and the strength of its named opponent, worldwide American imperialism.

These two portraits reveal that the strategies of assimilation and exclusion are entirely different reactions to group-based oppression. Assimilation depends upon one's ability to lose oneself, and exclusion relies upon one's visibility. Exclusion requires an outward identification with the group, while assimilation is a process of hiding the outward signs of a heritage.

There are similarities between the strategies of exclusion and assimilation, however, that reveal the outwardly and inwardly directed dilemmas of a threatened identity. Both are acts that deny and regain a social history. For the assimilated, the group history is shunned for the rewritten history of a progressive society. The excluded are pressured to conform to the image and history that institutional structures require; only with a radical strategy are they able to find a unique historical presence. Both exclusion and assimilation are efforts to deny who and what one is, either by a series of flights from reality (political suicide or romantic ideals), or by the taking on of disguises (new looks or new names). The outside appearance gains a self-reflective prominence as a means of converging one's own image of identity with others' image of one's identity. Being a victim of discrimination involves a play on exceptionality. For Rahel Varnhagen, the objective was to achieve exceptionality to prove she did not have the belittled status of a Jew. Malcolm X, through exceptionality, was able to frighten white institutions and break loose from their bonds by proving himself uncontrollable. It was through a lifetime struggle for exceptionality that these victims of discrimination attempted to find a place for themselves in society.

An Ethic of Survival

The attitude of the participants in this study toward their successes and failures is best described in Virginia's words: "The main measurement of success [was] basically survival." The ethic of survival means different things to different people, depending on how they define their responsibility and their basis for self-respect and how they view their struggles and needs.

Carmen's ethic of survival has been introduced in an earlier chapter. Carmen's goal is to maintain her sense of personal pride despite her partial resignation to failure. She holds on to her ability to "like herself" and to handle problems when they come along. Even though she feels vulnerable in terms of economic survival, she optimistically believes that "things will get better" and that, "God willing," she will pay her bills and "struggle through." Her responsibilities are to her children, and she feels satisfied if she is able to spend time with them and "try to make things better for them." She wants to help her children by enabling them to "think realistically," by encouraging them to achieve the kind of happiness possible in a life that imposes severe constraints on their opportunities. Her attitude toward her own survival makes Carmen's tolerance for discrimination on the job very high; it is in her home life that she is devoted to achieving dignity and competency.

John's ethic of survival is "making it through the rain." Like Carmen, his primary sense of responsibility is to his child, though one of his complaints about the ordeal of discrimination on the job is that it made him more irritable around his young daughter. John feels he has tolerated a series of discriminatory actions by his employer because he has a fairly high "breaking point." John believes that all persons have the responsibility to do the jobs their employers assign, because "they are the ones that give me my paycheck, you should do them right." When the employer is discriminatory, it does not change the basic requirements of the relationship: "What right does someone have to hassle me like that when I am doing my job? I took it from them, but I don't take it from very many individuals—they give me my paycheck; [with] individuals my boiling point is a little lower."

This sense of responsibility is revealed in the two ways in which he demonstrates his loyalty. First, despite opportunities to "steal from the company," John has "a little wishy-washy" code of honesty that prevents him. Second, he feels more loyalty to the employer than to the union, not because he believes the company serves his best interests, but "because the union can only help so much." He expects that if he filed a complaint with the union the company would investigate him and would find a reason to fire him, whether they had grounds or not. Even though he does not expect fair treatment from his employer, he has even less faith in his co-workers' support.

An important part of John's survival strategy is his self-sufficiency. When transferred to a new job, he had great difficulty with the paperwork required after truck deliveries. It was necessary for him, therefore, to teach himself the procedures and pick up things from other drivers. His overall philosophy is, "I don't need a lot." John does not attribute his ability to endure the strain of a discriminatory situation on the job to strength of character, but rather to his ability to "weather the storm." He compares himself unfavorably to a "strong person" like his brother, who willingly faced the struggles encountered by moving into a white neighborhood and has obtained the education that is necessary to "really move up." By his own estimation, in his weakness he endures: "My personality is what kept my job, my color created the problem. If it came to a point where I felt less than a man for taking the abuse, I would have quit; [as things were] if I had quit I would have felt less of myself."

Sylvia's ethic of survival permits her to see her own circumstances as favorable when compared with her peers' tragic lives. She is pleased that she has accomplished a lot, at least in comparison to others in the Latin community and to her family. Even though she grants that she has lost a great deal, owing to harassment in high school by black students, "If this didn't happen I would have a better education, I would have more friends, a better job, I would have been a different person." In a world where people "don't care" and "make excuses" instead of resolving differences, the only available strategy is to "care about oneself." She views her success in relative terms: she is not "on welfare," has not "been killed by a drug overdose," and has "graduated from high school." She attributes her low-paying job and inadequate housing to "competition." She advises herself not to think about a better life, because "then I am going to feel worse." "Like if I don't want to live here any more, then you feel frustrated because you can't move out of here."[27] She repeated several times during the interview that she has not suffered greatly from discrimination because she is bilingual, which she believes is often treated as an asset by her employers. This one socially valued trait, having bilingual skills, is constantly used as a reminder that society has granted her some "space" for advancement.

The ethic of survival for Clara is based upon personal resourcefulness rather than personal pride. Clara feels threatened by discriminatory policies only to the extent that they confuse personal worth with group stereotypes. Her unexpected battle against discrimination began when she discovered that she did not receive the same raise as male managers: "I was really hurt, because I knew the owner of the company real well and I didn't think it was fair." The reason she was "hurt" (in a way, that "wouldn't have mattered if they would have hired her at less") was that she originally felt it was a comment on her job performance. She describes her reasons for discussing the pay raise with her manager as "I just wanted him to tell me why. [His explanation was that he didn't want her salary at a higher level than two nonmanagement women with seniority.] I had my feelings hurt because I thought I was not doing as good a job as [the male managers] were, which wasn't the case at all, and I guess that kind of pacified me."

Clara feels she benefits from the discriminatory situation for several reasons. She received other compensation: she has use of a company car, and the boss has done "enormous favors" for her like offering her a loan. She also thinks discrimination undercuts other conflicts: "I think at one point the guys were upset because I was making the same amount of money they were. They felt like that because I was a woman . . . not that it was ever brought out into the open. I think they are a lot more satisfied now." The pay differential improves the attitude of her male co-workers, thereby saving her from subjection to covert discrimi- nation and jealousy. The manner in which Clara believes she will get ahead is to rely upon her personal appeal. She is not motivated to claim discrimination because "I think a lot of people might go against me. . . . I wouldn't want to ruin the relationships I do have there. Maybe that's not the kind of relationship to have, but that is the way it is, and I'm not going to change it." Clara chooses to tolerate the discrimination, even though it makes her feel "very classified" and angry whenever she thinks about it. She would be more assertive if her job were actually in jeopardy or if discrimination went beyond monetary penalties. For example, if she were sexually harassed, she wouldn't stand for it: "First of all, I would confront him. I don't know what the laws are, but I sure would find out." There is little nobility in Clara's ethic of survival. Her explanation for why changes are not made in society is that "people are lazy," as she is. Yet, as with several other victims of discrimination, her survival relies upon the primacy of the personal domain.

Virginia measures her own success in comparison with progress for women in society as a whole. Virginia was the "token female executive" in a stock brokerage firm, and when promoted she felt she did not get the salary to match her new title. She realized that the "general climate of the firm" was discriminatory, a function of attitudes both within the firm and of the clientele. She observed that her company "is very dependent upon the economy"; therefore, the environment was not conducive to creating opportunities for advancement or developing one's own sense of direction. To make a complaint would require "going through the channels of the corporate structure." She grew resigned to her defeat in the stock brokerage firm because she was "labeled a clerk"—a perception that was difficult to get beyond under the circumstances ("once a clerk, always a clerk").

Her efforts at fighting back did not involve direct action for fear of being labeled a troublemaker. For the short term she survived a relationship with her supervisor which was a "constant battle." She demonstrated her strength by quitting the job: "I am the only one I know who would have quit; they would have stuck with it. In fact, I know people who are still there [and they are making] the same old complaints. I have changed as far as my assertiveness goes. Now, I would grab those characters by the tie and say, 'hey, bozo—what's the problem?' I am feeling better off for having left; [otherwise] I would be still plodding away."

In her new job, Virginia is able to feel "more comfortable with myself." She is working where "equal opportunity exists; [which means that] they don't care what you are." Basically, she feels satisfied when she has "the same opportunity as everybody else." She has worked all her life to be self-sufficient and "equal": "I've worked hard, and I'm not giving it up for anything." In retrospect, it would be nice if they offered her her old job back and she could turn it down. But it is not that she "feels bad about [the experience]. . . . I think it helped me more than hurt me." Virginia sees social change as a slow process, and sometimes individuals are caught in the middle: "It is painful for the person involved [but without these sacrifices] others would not get the benefits and we wouldn't be able to see the changes. It is not worth it for the person, but eventually there will be a change in attitude." Virginia believes that at times she is sacrificed as an individual (in her struggle to keep her job during the time in her life when she was basically concerned with survival), and that at other times she benefits from social progress (when she eventually quit her job, continued her education in night school, and obtained a job in a company that is able to make room for the advancement of women). Virginia is sensitive to the fact that her needs are different from other people's: "My problems are very different from the little old lady down the stairs who is worried about her rent going up." Everyone's life problems are tied into the promotion of "some form of common good" for society as a whole.

Patricia has an exceptional ethic of survival as compared with others who perceive discrimination. Patricia does not accept that discrimination arises in isolated incidents (which in fact is imposed by the structure of the interview; she began our discussion by challenging that assumption). Patricia sees the experience of discrimination as a way of life. One incident that she offers as an example was her dismissal after working a short time as a receptionist in a nursing home. She was told her job performance was satisfactory, but was given a (later discovered) false explanation for her layoff (that her position was being eliminated). She assumes that the incident happened because they were desperate to hire someone but could not wait for a "qualified white person." When she unexpectedly returned to pick up her final check and found her replacement, her supervisor was obviously embarrassed. Patricia did not confront her; she "gave her a look and kept going." In the long term, she has tried to "forget about it like a nightmare you don't want to remember."

Patricia believes that in most cases racial motives for discrimination are obvious: "They ask you *those* kind of questions." But she avoids confrontation because "I don't have the tools to deal with it." She has an Asian co-worker on her present job who empathizes with the black situation because "the whole population does not see us the way we are." She classifies some situations in life as inherently discriminatory. As a phone company employee she dealt with restrictions that went beyond discrimination to the "ludicrous." The phone company was an institution that epitomized "not understanding what being a woman was all about." The company "looked at us and determined our needs," and it all seemed "logical and necessary to them."

Patricia distinguishes between choosing to avoid confrontations and engaging in struggles. Discrimination cases rarely become struggles, simply because "discrimination cases do not go to court." Her own potential to engage in struggle is somewhere between "passive and militant." She is not like her brother, who has chosen to be one of the few black residents of a white community and who is determined not to move, even after being subjected to property damage and physical threats. During the 1960s, which in her mind was a period of progress, she belonged to a radical black political organization but felt they "never achieved the ends I thought necessary." Her personal philosophy centers on the idea that life is about "choices." She feels she has had more choices than others and is worried about the average person who is unaware of choices because "their life is six blocks long." She is committed to her profession, community health care services, because she wants to "in a small way make a difference in black women's lives." By opening up choices for others, she hopes to help them find their self-esteem.

Patricia is exceptional because she is not only surviving but is extending life choices to others. How does this reconcile with her total surrender to incidents of discrimination? This is Patricia's world view: "I can't blame the individual; society as a whole has perpetuated that kind of [discrimination] and it hasn't died." She individualizes the incident, but not without attributing a societal cause. She surmounts each instance of discrimination, yet extreme anger persists. The stress builds, a condition she feels she shares with other blacks: "Sometimes I wonder why black people don't go crazy with all that multiple stress."[28] She believes that even though her freedom may be very limited, "there is some, so I have to value what little I have and [use the freedom] to choose what I want to be."

These portrayals illustrate how victims of discrimination protect themselves from the hardships imposed by relying upon an illusive and private honor. Their sense of honor or pride, seen in the context of how they create opportunities and constraints within an ethic of survival, justifies submitting their personal needs to the demands of powerful institutions. Thus, the victim of discrimination upholds the appearance of justice, even within a system that denies equality. The victim's ethics are maintained within an individual, self-defined realm. Institutional and bureaucratic grievance procedures invade this personal ethic and strengthen the illusion that institutions are fair and that discrimination is not prevalent as long as the victims of discrimination believe that their individual misfortunes stem from the acts of aberrant individuals and from business practices.[29] Honor subdues aggression, as in John's commitment to honest dealings with a firm that maintains racially discriminatory business practices. Pride subdues powerlessness, as in Carmen's need to "like herself" when she is powerless to combat pay differentials she acknowledges as unfair.[30] When neither institutional practices nor the law of equal opportunity affirms a moral commitment to standards, victims of discrimination cannot find purpose beyond their individual fate.[31]

Blinded by the ethic of survival, individuals become satisfied with limited expectations of equal treatment.[32] Equality is not seen as universally attainable; radically egalitarian values may be supported on the primary dimension of private life and sacrificed in the realms of work, education, and housing. Carmen, for example, accepts inequality as a worker because of the scarcity of jobs. At home, however, a husband who does not assume equal responsibility for the family is unacceptable. These expectations allow individuals to accept their mistreatment as the result of personal misfortune rather than as based in structural inequalities.[33] Working in an egalitarian environment, for example, is like being born into a good family. As already mentioned, Virginia's definition of a fair employer is someone who "doesn't care who you are." Working under Betty's discriminatory employer was "like being a robot. They feed you all this rot. . .we don't care about what your personal life is, we don't care about how you are affected by it, all we want is the work." In her present job, where she has not experienced discrimination, the atmosphere is more like being part of a "family." In one instance, a positive company attitude was seen as a means of deterring discriminatory practices. When Nora looked for a new job after her discrimination dispute, she considered it important to reveal why she left the old job in order to inform any prospective employer that she would not tolerate discrimination. The distinction between sterile and congenial environments is not based upon the normative criterion of fairness; it reflects the need for security, comfort, and recognition found within a group of people like oneself.

Survival is about the capacity to endure real sacrifices. As observers of these people's lives, we must respect their difficult choices about the pain they wish to surmount or avoid in their lives. Their decisions depend partly on their circumstances, yet are ultimately decided as value questions. How much will I give up for success? How much responsibility do I have to myself and others? Is this issue more important to me than other struggles I encounter? Any interpretation must appreciate decisions made by victims of discrimination to protect what they value most.

Timeless notions of justice and right may not bring about justice in a person's lifetime. The requirements imposed upon victims of discrimination may make it realistic for them not to pursue claims. The loosely defined right of equal protection is concretely realized in everyday conflicts. As the sociologist Richard Sennett explains: "[T]he rhythm of growth and decay in life is not the rhythm of growth and decay of society. There is an unbridgeable gap—or, to put it positively, each of us can re-imagine authority privately as we cannot in public. We have a principle by which to criticize society based not on abstract deduction about justice and right but on our intimate knowledge of time."[34] Thus, the assessment of antidiscrimination policies ultimately rests upon the force of rights when actualized in social relations. The civil rights society poses a theory of rights that anticipates that making a claim is an empowering mechanism.[35] The power of rights depends upon the probability that the state will enforce one's demands. Thus, as victims of discrimination struggle to realize their will, they employ the concept of right, as if it were a resource available to them, in order to enhance their life chances.[36] Individuals' chances for survival are affected by the "origin, decay, and change of rights in society" in the same way as lives are enhanced by changes in resources and opportunities.[37]

The power of right, however, is lost in controversies in which people with limited resources make claims of prejudicial treatment. The ethic of survival becomes an impoverished substitute for the pursuit of ideals. For people to see the invocation of rights as an extension of their will, they must go beyond the private dignity found within an ethic of survival to the expression of a public cause or goal.

The Politicization of Private Honor

At the level of doctrinal debates, the test of good race policies is often posed as the congruence between antidiscrimination policies and democratic ideals. The expansion of the equal protection doctrine is supported by legal reasoning that demonstrates that increased governmental intervention furthers society's commitment to public purposes. In school desegregation cases, a crucial issue is the historical transformation of public education to promote federal and state governmental purposes.[38] In voting rights cases, the interests of minorities are deemed fundamental because of the integral role of participation (in local primaries, for example) for the proper functioning of the national governmental process.[39] And in general, the responsibility assumed by the courts is to assure that political practices reflect American ideals through a repudiation of the racial distinctions based "solely on ancestry," because such distinctions are "odious to a free people whose institutions are based on a doctrine of equality."[40] The expansion of antidiscrimination law, according to the model of legal protection, fuses together ideal and practice.

Those who fight for and win group-based struggles, either directly or vicariously, are sometimes able to identify antidiscrimination doctrine with a public purpose. Since the 1950s, the focus of civil rights activities that has promoted the most intragroup and interracial cooperation has been the expansion of black voting rights. Probably voting rights is the civil rights issue that has gained the broadest support in the white community, although the violations still continue, because these efforts do not directly threaten the "private" and economic interests of whites. The voting rights cases are an exceptional development in antidiscrimination law, however, because these rights are closely knit into the political apparatus; in the abstract sense, legal and political identity converge. Most discrimination complaints in everyday life rest in the gray area, inextricably linked to a system of economic inequalities, where the identification of political purposes may be troublesome and difficult to achieve.

The progress made in the courts and by civil rights activists creates an impression of legal action that is discordant with victims' potential responses to everyday instances of discrimination. These everyday situations do not conform to the ideal of legal protection, in which the interests of the community would be served by each person's employing the law to preserve the integrity of her or his individual domain. The experiences of those interviewed show that we cannot expect antidiscrimination law to protect the individual by deterring prejudicial treatment in private settings. If John, for example, could use his "rights" to end his harassment, the law would have some effectiveness in his case. Yet this is contrary to reality; the victims in this study only dared speak of the law as a deterrent "jokingly."[41] In the analysis of these social conflicts it has become obvious that the potential of the law to grant "rights" that can be individually exercised is not realized unless the complainant stages an all-out battle against discrimination.

Another way rights-based litigation could be effective is through the transformation of individual interests into group causes by civil rights activists and organizations. Issues become politicized when groups identify conflict between their goals and the state,[42] then translate their grievances into group- or class-based interests. The identification of group interests, as discussed in Chapter 1, is seen as antithetical to the ideology of antidiscrimination law. The expansion of equal protection law has been designed to create instruments that vindicate individual rather than collective rights. As will be discussed further in the next chapter, these individuals are caught within their ambivalence between group and individual identity, and their ethic of survival most often does not permit them to affirm their group consciousness (either race and gender difference or class distinctions, e.g., workers or tenants). But contrary to the experience of these individuals, in the contemporary civil rights society issues of race and sex appear to be highly politicized.

The intense political interest in a social problem can blur adversarial relations and mute political resistance rather than promote political change. Citizen participation in social programs during the Great Society, for example, was made to appear desirable, yet relieved anxieties and created a beneficent image of the authorities who imposed controls.[43] Political interest in environmental, consumer, nuclear war, and welfare issues rises and falls in cyclical patterns that produce temporary cathartic release of concerns but fall short of initiating social change.[44] In the long run, the civil rights society's image of group action may have, in a similar fashion, created a cathartic relief, both for the majority and for those who are subject to prejudicial treatment, that satisfies individual notions of justice without fueling the potential for change.

Without a concept of group rights to give meaning to their injustices, the people who experience discrimination are denied their self-respect. With the "depersonalization of public and social life," they are caught in what Hannah Arendt terms the "modern loss of respect." In a world without a meaningful sense of what is public, we are "closed within ourselves, we would never be able to forgive ourselves any failing or transgression because we would lack the experience of the person for the sake of whom one can forgive."[45] The failure of these people to see their conflict in terms of rights leaves the dispute unresolved. These are victims without a cause. The interviews showed a great variety of responses to the question, "What would make you feel redeemed?" Some believe in appropriate revenge: I wish they could be put in my shoes and "then they could see what it feels like." Others would not like to see the person responsible fired, because "he is doing what most people would do. . .it would be an overreaction. What needs to happen is for him to change his outlook." Several were concerned about others "going through the same thing" but did not feel they had done anything to prevent that. Carol suggests that "it would be nice to get an apology. It would make me feel a little better." Consistent in their responses was the feeling that they were at a loss to find meaning and purpose in a series of incidents that have severely disrupted their lives.

In the next chapter I develop a more complete explanation for why victims choose not to perceive discriminatory events in terms of legal wrongs. We have seen that the law is weak compared to the bonds of victimhood. Therefore, people adopt a stoic stance because their only choice is to endure injustice. Yet in the next chapter we find further reason why victims are discouraged from employing antidiscrimination law because the law engenders reactions which in turn defeat its effective use.

Six / Legality Enters Life

The basic assumption underlying the model of legal protection is that the law is a powerful tool that can be employed by victims to deter perpetrators from discriminatory practices. Since the model is effective only if victims are willing to recognize and report violations, there is an implicit assumption that as long as the rational calculation of costs and benefits favors legal action, victims will perceive litigation as an attractive recourse.

How do people view the law? Although social scientists have had sporadic interest in this question, the way in which it has been asked has predetermined the range of answers. Those beginning from the paradigm of legal protection are interested in how attitudes promote legal effectiveness. Hypothetically, the victims are the beneficiaries of the law, and its legitimacy rests on their faith in the law's ability to serve their needs. Thus, if the law is ineffective, the cause lies in the inadequacies found in the intended beneficiaries: individuals' lack of information and knowledge about their rights and their limited resources for using legal channels (money, information, availability of lawyers, etc.).[1]

There have been attempts to pose the question of attitudes toward the law without the bias imposed by the model of legal protection.[2] These approaches transform the methodology from measuring the attitudes that people have about the legal system to understanding strategies for responding to unjust treatment from the viewpoint of the layperson. Since my perspective on mass consciousness attempts to recognize the knowledge of the subjects (as discussed in Chapter 2) I anticipated that the responses of persons to the law reflect powerful images created by the ideology of legal protection as well as the circumstances of their social experience. Throughout, my study has introduced the victim's perspective, which emerges from confronting the paradoxes and ambiguities associated with the law.[3]

I find that from the victim's point of view there are strong barriers to perceiving their problem as discrimination and establishing a claim as legitimate. The psychological needs of victims work against their transforming the dispute into a public cause. People view the law as both protective and destructive; they fear that if they seek a legal resolution, they will not gain power but instead will lose control over a hostile situation. They resolve the ambiguity by deciding to reject the relevance of law to their lives.

The Victim's View of the Law

Claiming Discrimination

As previously argued, in order for an individual to press a claim that unfavorable treatment stems from discriminatory practices, it is necessary to assume the role of the victim. The public claim of discrimination, even though one may be certain of the perpetrator's motives, is expressed uneasily because, paradoxically, the words force a person to become a victim in order to assert a right. The ambivalent invocation of the concept of discrimination stultifies legal action.

In this study, those interviewed discussed the discrimination they experienced in qualified terms. Some approached it by denying self-involvement: "Sometimes I don't even feel like I was personally being discriminated against, as if they did not know who I was or saw who I was." Another approach characterized acts of discrimination as the result of personal likes and dislikes. As one respondent commented, "It was discriminatory to a degree, but also a personal situation." Others distinguished between believing discrimination had occurred and calling it discrimination in front of others (friends or the perpetrator). As a woman engaged in an employment dispute explained, "I talked about the situation with everybody I came in contact with...[but as] far as calling it discrimination, [to] no one." Another woman was sure that her race and welfare status were factors influencing the denial of her rental application, but that did not mean that she would make a "complaint to [the landlords] about discrimination."

To experience discrimination, by these accounts, is to sense one's own invisibility and to grasp the reality of differential treatment. These individuals perceived that neither the mistreatment nor their response to it focused on a deliberate attack against them, but injustices resulted from being discounted or ignored.

One reason why people are hesitant about making a claim of discrimination is because they expect that legal authorities will demand the verification of their word with concrete evidence. They place a low value on their subjective knowledge in relation to other forms of objective knowledge produced by corporations and bureaucracies and presented in formal documents. Thus, these individuals internalize the leap between the actual occcurrence of discrimination and its empirical proof. In fact, they are reluctant to come forward with a complaint based only on their word because they fear they will be accused of attributing unreasonable authority to one's own position. These explanations for not pressing the issue of discrimination often made reference to the unsubstantiated nature of their cases: "everything is verbal"; "no formal bookkeeping or job descriptions"; "everything went on behind closed doors, nobody heard what I asked him." When these individuals are immobilized by their low regard for their own judgments of the cause of the dispute, they not only prematurely resign themselves to their failure to establish the burden of proof, but they are forced to accept the authoritative account of what happened. For example, the organizational opponent, an employer, may have greater access to objective evidence because of routine record keeping or established procedures. One woman professed that her potential employer was not "discriminating" when he refused to hire females to care for mental patients at night because "he was approaching it from an administrative point of view." John, who was upset by the appearance that he was violating numerous "regulations," found that his supervisor was quick to "write him up" for infractions, "but they never fired me. Even though they had all this *evidence*." Indeed, he was intimidated by the collection of "evidence," even though he knew the reports contained frivolous charges against him. Nora believed that the only way potential litigants could prove their claims was to beat the employer in the game of collecting papers, documents, memos, and tape recordings. The perceived requirement for evidence, in the form of the supervisor's written report or other forms of documentation, is ironic given these individuals' ability based on their own intuition and broader view of the relationship, to reach their own self-evident conclusions of discriminatory treatment. Furthermore, this reasoning shifts the focus of responsibility for the perpetrator's wrongdoing to inevitable consequences of official policy.

Another source of ambivalence about claiming discrimination is their sense that nobody has taken deliberate action against them. When they retrospectively evaluate the incident in the context of an ongoing relationship, these people often find themselves unable to link the harm experienced to the direct action of the perpetrators. For several respondents, the sequence of events did not focus on the perpetrator because they were provoked into reacting defensively. Betty, who was eventually fired, stated: "What I had noticed is that other people around me with less time [in the company] had advanced....They were making it really difficult for me to do my work...and how can they tell me how to do my [own] work? So I did it my way." Betty, embittered by what she perceived as her employer's interference, provoked further antagonism. In her opinion, her poor performance was a consequence of their unwillingness to advance her in the job. John had a clearer understanding of the conflict: "What they did is put me in a position where I wanted to quit." Other respondents found that discriminatory situations involve a series of small incidents; thus, in order to make a complaint, the individual would be forced to emphasize and seemingly exaggerate a history of events. One woman said that discriminatory activity continues precisely because "people like me wait too long to do something." When the conflict finally surfaces, oftentimes the person who feels wronged has taken the unsettling action. The victim is confused because the sequence of events does not conform to the pattern of perpetrator-initiated activity that is implied in the model of legal protection. It is also difficult for the victim to arrive at a reasonable explanation of why it is "them" and not "me."

The legal concept of discrimination has a historical and analytical basis in the identification with a group cause. To put this concept into operation, so to speak, involves finding a basis for the claim in terms of the individual's group identity. Yet, these respondents resist perceiving their situation as the result of their group identity. In some cases, they depersonalize their mistreatment rather than identify with the group fate: "[discrimination] depends upon who you are working for; changes in supervisors [solve the problem]"; "[discrimination] occurred because he has a problem and I was sort of a scapegoat." Or, "I expected [discrimination]; that's the way men treat women." These statements disassociate the individual who experiences discrimination from group identity, causes, or concerns, either by emphasizing the idiosyncratic nature of the perpetrator's actions or by universalizing the presence of discrimination. Several respondents supported these rationalizations by pointing out that everyone is vulnerable to some type of discrimination. A black man explained: "I don't walk around with my head buried in the sand. People discriminate against anything and anybody." Two respondents referred to discrimination directed at their "fat relatives" as examples of the prevalence of discrimination. A few even attempted to defend discrimination as unavoidable: "I even discriminate against Mexicans." In sum, the respondents felt that it was self-defeating to associate an illogical and irrational process of mistreatment with a real cause. When one woman did state her claim in terms of group concerns, she met resistance: "Most of the people I talked to thought I overreacted [when I complained of discrimination]...[I think it was] because I was labeled a feminist."

Even though these individuals express ambivalence about publicly claiming discrimination, they believe they have been seriously harmed.

Their ambivalence places them in a self-imposed trap: they struggle with an image of themselves and their actions which produces an uncomfortable sense of exceptionality. While antidiscrimination law ostensibly promotes dignity and universal human rights, in practice individuals may prefer the dignity found in their anonymity to an attempt to exercise their rights under such law.

Why does a public claim of discrimination require the transformation of feelings of anger and injustice into the language of rights? When we examine the language of the law we often find that the meaning of a word is found in its usage. Thus, the words *justice* and *right* have meaning in reference to "standards."[4] When persons employ the language of rights, they imply standards of judgment found in institutional rules and social ideals. People who experience mistreatment search for standards to justify their proclamation of rights. But, individuals who both protect their individuality and deny their exceptionality cannot make claims on the basis of the violation of good or bad standards; they can only speak to the legitimacy of their own feelings. Victims thus lose the potential for the language of rights to acknowledge their feelings in a public realm. The power of rights as a potential source of redemption for the otherwise powerless, a positive gesture that reaches out to those similarly situated, is diffused by the consciousness of the civil rights society.

The retreat to anonymity is a direct result of the hollowness of antidiscrimination rights. The standards reflected in antidiscrimination law are "evolving" and conform to "present practices." The application of the law, moreover, does not serve the intrinsic interests of the oppressed group: the law is not designed to protect the black, woman, or minority person, it protects the hypothetical "equal person." Tocqueville warned that democratic freedom can silence the proclamation of right: "the body is left free and the soul is enslaved." The "master" says: "You are free to think differently from me, and to retain your life, your property, and all that you possess; but you are henceforth a stranger among your people. You may retain your civil rights, but they will be useless to you, for you will never be chosen by your fellow-citizens. . . .You will remain among men, but you will be deprived of the rights of mankind."[5] The claim of right, Tocqueville explains, brings with it the severest sanction in a democratic society.

The reluctance to move beyond the perception of discrimination to formally claim the protection of antidiscrimination law is partly due to a resistance to the negative image of the victim. Moreover, this ambivalence deflects potential conflict because the individual chooses not to categorize mistreatment within narrow boundaries of discriminatory activity, thereby accepting the power of law but restricting its domain.

The reluctance to cross the boundary between normalcy and victim-hood forces the victim to justify the perpetrator's actions. Those who cross the boundary experience sanctions—the label of the victim (the powerless outsider) or the label of a group stereotype (the potential zealot).

The role of victim assumed by those who advocate rights coincides with other roles: employee, gender, citizen; and the social construction of these roles creates expectations about proper behavior. Respondents fear that claiming discrimination will interfere with "getting the job done," "providing for your family," or "being treated like a woman." Making the claim of discrimination forces the individual to make a choice between appropriate role behaviors where the more productive response is to choose other roles more crucial to one's life orientation. The role of the victim is the strategy of last resort.

The Intruding Presence in Everyday Life

Despite the fact that victims are reluctant to use the law, they cling to the belief that it benefits them. Helen explained that when she was asked to report her age on an employment application, "I told her I thought you weren't asking that any more." She also indicated that she was sure she could "report her. . . right then and there." She knew that "they weren't supposed to consider your religion, age, your color, or whatever the heck it was, and she sure did." All the respondents, when asked if they felt the law was on their side in the dispute, suggested that, at least in principle, the law would have supported their position. For example, one respondent involved in a housing dispute explained: "I knew I had the right. It made me feel good, that I knew if I wanted to [I could make a claim]." Two respondents explicitly mentioned how the law "in principle," if not in the particular dispute could benefit them. Delma suggested that the law "is irrelevant on a day to day basis; there is not a lot you can do. In extreme cases, just the fact that it exists, you can say there are laws against that sort of thing, you can say that jokingly. . . . Just the fact [the law] exists is to my advantage." The implication is that the law is ineffective in the formal resolution of claims, but that legal authority can be called upon as a joke, in order to make a point without creating tension in the work environment. Virginia also has found the law "irrelevant" to the resolution of her grievance, yet feels that the law is "effective just by being around. I wouldn't have my [new] job without it. I wouldn't be able to obtain credit." Both acknowledge that at some level, apart from the enforce-ment of claims, antidiscrimination law has an effect on their treatment as members of a class.

Several respondents, when speaking of the law in principle, did not explicitly admit to their own failures to "protect" their rights. They credit their own behavior as consistent with the "full pursuit" of their rights, regardless of actual efforts to establish a claim. One woman who did not persist in her complaint carefully noted, "I think I know my rights; I'll take them to the limit." Another made this assurance, in retrospect: "[I would] take it to court as a matter of principle." There is a strong conviction among almost all of the disputants that the law in "absolute" terms would rectify the injustices done to them; but they could only speak hypothetically because they had not tested the law to its limit.

Their assumption that there are absolute guarantees in the law in principle seems to contradict their attitudes toward the law once it is employed. After they initiated legal action or even considered invoking it, the respondents saw legal resolution as a risky course of action. They feared that legal intervention would worsen their situation.

The prospect of legal intervention has heightened a sense of powerlessness and produced a fear of loss of control.[6] Nora believes that the decision to go to court was like opening up "Pandora's box."

Fear of the law may stem from the prospect of having to reconstruct the events in court. For some, the fear was provoked by the seriousness of the legal aspect. As Carol explains, the law is not ineffective: "People, they are just afraid to stand up." Delma describes her feelings: "I might have taken it to court; I might have done that. I went to the [unemployment office] and she confronted me and I felt so helpless. It was just his word against mine, and I am dumb. . .and there is nothing I can do." The unemployment office was a preview of the confrontation in court, where she would feel exposed, forced to defend herself with nothing other than her own words and intelligence.

Victims of discrimination also fear that their powerlessness will be accentuated in court because the legal process will address only a part of the problem. As one respondent reasons, the law will "not represent personality: it is cut and dry—there [is] no room for emotion." Behavior and loyalties may change when allies are asked to participate in legal proceedings: "[Going to court] would mean that people would have to speak up. In the lounge they might say you are really getting screwed. To say that in a court of law is different. When your neck is on the chopping block, you ain't going to start talking."

These feelings may be reinforced by the belief that legal power is fundamentally corrupt. Careful distinctions are often made, however, between the authority of the "law" and court officials. One respondent feels that the outcome in a legal case depends on "who is on the bench." When asked about the effectiveness of antidiscrimination law, John responds: "You're dealing with personalities and attitudes, not just the law. The whole judicial system is manipulated by attitudes of those in power." Helen, when speaking of law in general, believes there should be stronger enforcement powers backing the law, yet she finds the actual authority of the police and other legal officials abusive. Thus, faith in the law is often mixed with distrust of the agents of legal bureaucracies.

Legal intervention also had the effect of restructuring the conflict, according to respondents, by provoking extreme hostility. The respondents claim that they avoided legal action in order to maintain civilities or remain employed: "If I didn't want to work there any more, then I think I would take legal action"; I would not "fight to the principle" unless all was lost, "unless they fired me, because I'm not knocking down the world"; or if I sued for sexual harassment, "I will lose my job, as simple as that." When the law is effective, it is at best a "stopgap" measure, to use when defeat is already certain to salvage a situation after one is resigned to failure. As in Betty's case, the "guy from the EEOC" told her, "I'd help you this time, but they're out to get you." In her case, the law can only delay what she perceives as the "inevitable revenge" of the personnel department; she would at most achieve a small victory before her ultimate dismissal.

Several respondents revealed that when they were confronted with the prospect of initiating a legal action they worried about their own guilt, as if they were charged with criminal offenses. Delma, while considering whether to file a complaint, mused, "Maybe it is me, maybe I am doing something wrong." Laura, who precipitated an act of violence, after which she lost her job, reflected: "What I had done was against the rules, but what she had done was also against the rules. I didn't take legal action against it because I knew I had done a wrong part, I didn't try to take away from what I had done." John also revealed his feeling of guilt once he discovered himself singled out for discriminatory treatment. He felt as if his whole life were on trial; he was always on the defensive and compelled to prove he was doing his best possible work.

More generally, these victims felt it was necessary to prevent the law from aggravating their situations.[7] Often this meant blocking the law from taking over the relative normalcy of day-to-day life. As Carmen said, "What was important to me at the time was trying to erase the situation. I was split between the idea of pursuing it in court and just letting it die. I couldn't stand the stress." Another woman explained, "The situation is really blocked out, because I don't want them to take action against me."

Images of Legality

The view of law held by these respondents is in stark contrast to the anticipated response of victims to protective law. The collection of statements by individuals who feel they have experienced discrimination
creates a composite picture of responses to legality analogous to the
responses of Joseph K. in Kafka's *The Trial*. The victims of discrimination view the invocation of the law with fear, guilt, and a heightened
dread of destruction.

Joseph K., after being "arrested" unexpectedly one morning, is concerned with maintaining the order of his life by establishing boundaries between the legal investigation and his mundane daily routine as
a bank clerk. Joseph K.'s guilt, shame, and embarrassment lead him and
others to conclude he has been arrested on "criminal" charges. After
his first interrogation by the "Court," he is appalled by the corruption
and incompetence of the officials; his first reaction is that either his
own knowledge of the "Law in the books" or reform of the Court will
enhance his chance for acquittal. But on the advice of others, he relies
upon lawyers, who boast of their own importance and indispensability.
The use of lawyers, he is told, is not a strategy that will lead to his
acquittal, but it will produce delay and detachment from the Court
and its officials. The plot of *The Trial* proceeds with Joseph K.'s own
curiosity driving him to his entanglement with the Law. The Court
wants "nothing from him";[8] it is only a mirror of his own desires.

The Trial is a parable about law, where Law is both universal (in that
it is unavoidable) and powerless (in that it cannot absolve guilt). The
delusions of the law are revealed in the story of the doorkeeper:
"[B]efore the Law stands a doorkeeper. To this doorkeeper there comes
a man from the country who begs for admittance to the Law."[9] The
doorkeeper cannot admit the man and keeps him waiting, until the
man notices the "radiance of the Law" as a light within the door. Then
the doorkeeper shuts the door. The "doorkeeper gave the message of
salvation to the man only when it could no longer help him."[10] The
doorkeeper who represents the officials of the Law is a distraction
produced by the man's desperate desire to pursue the Law. The doorkeeper is not involved in "simple deception"; the only deception is the
belief that the Law will resolve the man's guilt.

Erich Heller describes the search of Kafka's hero for the truth as a
distorted analogy to Plato's passage in *The Republic* in which the prisoner in a cave sees shadows on the wall as reality:

> [P]erfectly aware of his wretched imprisonment and obsessed with a
> monomaniac desire to know, the prisoner has, by his unruly behaviour and
> his incessant entreaties, provoked the government of his prison to an act of

malicious generosity. In order to satisfy his passion for knowledge they have covered the walls with mirrors which, owing to the curved surface of the cave, distort what they reflect. Now the prisoner sees lucid pictures, definite shapes, clearly recognizable faces, an inexhaustible wealth of detail. His gaze is fixed no longer on empty shades, but on a full reflection of ideal reality.[11]

The distorting mirrors in the cave correspond to the distortion created by protective law for the modern victim. The victim's own quest for truth, the attainment of justice for the excluded, is provoked (or has been encouraged) by the act of "malicious generosity" that has designed a futile path that will not ultimately lead to justice.[12]

Those who experience discrimination are subjected to no "simple deception" by acts of malicious generosity. Kafka asks the reader to enter his theater of the absurd where Joseph K. wakes up one morning and the world is not as expected. Kafka introduces the reader to a double paradox—Joseph K.'s frustrating question about the Law and the reader's frustration in understanding the meaning of Joseph K.'s quest with the law. The reader finds meaning by watching Joseph K. go through an imaginary maze. Or the reader is drawn into the paradox by asking the wrong questions: What is the Court of Inquiry? Is Joseph K. guilty? or, Why is this nightmare happening to him? By analogy, the fallacies of legal protection become obvious after the reader rejects the wrong questions and realizes that the victim has become immobilized by the Law's paradoxes.

Victims of discrimination are attracted to the "radiance of the Law." They often feel reassured because antidiscrimination law exists. Since their need to resolve their sense of injustice draws them to evoke legal themes, they feel a sense of guilt and estrangement. Like Joseph K. they are overcome by hopelessness; they treat their own desire to use legal channels as a destructive obsession. Joseph K. criticized his own need to pursue his case: "[I]f I had behaved sensibly, nothing further would have happened, all this would have been nipped in the bud. But one is so unprepared."[13] The solution for the victims of discrimination is to reestablish boundaries that push legality away from their everyday lives.

Whatever model is applied to take account of the incompatibility of law with everyday life, when people are alienated from the law—as victims in the shadow of the law—they rely on personal strengths or sources of authority outside of the legal realm. Thus, individuals may choose to do nothing to resolve their grievances because taking action may destroy the option of relying on their own devices of personal protection. When disputes become polarized because of the introduction of the language of rights, people may lose ground in continuing relationships that are unfriendly stand-offs or may be forced into painful contact with perpetrators that can be avoided with seemingly minor inconvenience (e.g., holding out in an undesirable job or avoiding a hostile landlord).

The consequences of avoiding legal discourse must be evaluated in the context of the power structure in which the conflict arises. When the equilibrium of perpetrator and victim relationships is destroyed and the redemption of rights unlikely, the outcome of the conflict is likely either to reinforce or to worsen preexisting power inequalities.

An important issue remains: how does the avoidance of law impose other, nonlegal means of power on the conflict? In other words, what are the implications of the coexistence of an abiding faith in the law to resolve discrimination conflicts and the strong predisposition to avoid the intervention of law in our lives? Throughout this study, I have begun to answer this question by showing how this paradox of a civil rights society operates in nonobvious ways to encourage people to accept unequal treatment they believe to be caused by their personal failures.

Seven / Conclusion: Voices Excluded from the Law

The results of my interviews show that people who have experienced discriminatory treatment resist engagement in legal tactics because they stand in awe of the power of the law to disrupt their daily lives. At the same time, they are cynical about the power of the law actually to help them secure the jobs, housing, and other opportunities they lay claim to. They fear that, if they seek a legal resolution, they will not improve their position but will lose control of a hostile situation. These repondents also feel that asserting their legal rights would not enable them to express their sense of dignity but would force them to justify their worthiness against a more powerful opponent. Injured persons reluctantly employ the label of discrimination because they shun the role of the victim. Therefore, they choose to rely on strategies for economic and personal survival that perpetuate their victimization but are seen as more desirable than submitting to the terms of legal discourse.

This version of the victim's view of the law resonates with the exhaustion and anger directed at strategies of legal reform in communities outside of the mainstream of American society. But the disenchantment of feminist and race-conscious groups has long been ignored in academic and legal scholarship on equal protection. One reason why I offer a different view of legal reform is simply because I have listened to the stories of persons from racial, economic, and gender groups that are rarely included in the samples for academic analysis. This has enabled comparisons among an unusual group of people, ranging economically from the middle class to the extremely poor and including a disproportionate number of women. Although the people in these interviews have eloquently expressed themselves and have shown enormous insight about their own situations, we should be cautious and tentative about our interpretations because dissimilar life experiences and social identities may have hindered us from fully appreciating their words.

But these stories do not gain the importance they deserve without putting them into a context that can amplify their voices in relation to the resounding chorus of progressive legal reform. Despite the expectation of discontinuities between the ideal and the practice of legal reform, there are not simply "flaws in the system": the model of legal protection deters social victims from liberating themselves from oppressive conditions.

First, the model of legal protection does not present a viable option for social change, because law is not central to most people's lives. My study brings to light the realities of victimhood dimmed by the paternal optimism of legal solutions. Conventional legal analysis magnifies the authority of legal rules vis-à-vis other social roles. These in-depth portrayals of responses to discrimination illustrate how the links between economic, social, psychological, sexual, and legal roles create an ethic of survival which conflicts with the protective role of law. The law is incapable of providing protection when people are caught in bureaucratic entanglements and experience less risk by holding onto competing role conceptions: sole provider of a family, loyal employee, passive woman, marginal member of the labor force, or responsible citizen. My findings inform the critique of the role of law in the modern welfare state, supporting, for example, Claus Offe's argument that the effectiveness of law as an instrument of social change has been limited with the growth of the bureaucratic state. As positive law has become devoid of moral content and reduced to abstract and empty phrases, the application of law either is not flexible enough to deal with the complexity of social and economic problems or is interpreted in an "ad-hoc, context dependent fashion." As I have shown, the principles of equal protection are undermined once they are applied in the concrete setting of business, school, or rental agency because the claimant does not defend a moral principle. Moreover, legal regulations are often ineffective because their enforcement depends on positive and negative incentives that assume that both parties make "exchange-like" rational calculations. Offe argues that people will "escape" from the calculated reasoning imposed by the law because they prefer to "relate to each other as reasonable persons" and not place themselves under the threat of the state.[1] This tendency appears to be particularly strong in race and gender disputes, as demonstrated by my respondents' unwillingness to subject themselves to the form of problem solving offered by the law and their discomfort with actions that disrupt commonly held understandings of proper behavior.

Second, my findings raise questions that go beyond the failure of implementing the model of legal protection by suggesting that strengthening the rule of law may not empower victims. The hostile image of the law held by respondents considering legal recourse is a harsh reality compared to the spirit of protective law that promises to give purpose and justice to its beneficiaries' lives. In contemporary American society it is typically assumed that the "rule of law" is strengthened by the increase in enforcement powers, the clarification of goals, or the elimination of discretion, so that the right-bearer is protected. Yet when people contemplate invoking the right of "equal treatment under law," they find themselves in a position with only undesirable alternatives. The bonds of victimhood are reinforced rather than broken by the intervention of legal discourse.

Yet, given this critique of the model of legal protection, is the language of rights inherently disempowering? Rights are not self-enforcing; they are realized within a social context. Those who proclaim rights provided by antidiscrimination law may pay the cost of accepting abnormality, defeat, and a demeaning group stereotype. But for those who avoid a negative self-image, their ambivalence toward making a legal claim creates a powerful bond to discrimination. By an act of choice people accept narrow boundaries of the meaning of discrimination and remain unsure about the cause of the injustices they have encountered. Victims justify their own inaction by exaggerating the tyrannical power of their opponents (exclusion). Confusion and self-blame (distortion) diffuse their anger. In fact, they fear their own anger and choose to repress their violent reactions to experiencing wrongful treatment through what they perceive as the more honorable act of self-control. Victims accept a heroic ethic of survival, justifying their own passivity as a positive and socially acceptable response to discrimination (sacrifice).

Minorities and women assume a role more like the accused defendant in a criminal trial than like the ally of government prosecutors. In criminal trials, for example, the proceedings become a formality, cases are processed with the assumption of the defendant's guilt, and the ideology of procedural justice contradicts the practice of bargained justice. This creates a dilemma for the criminal justice system, which must satisfy external demands for due process treatment of defendants. The situation of criminal defendants, as described by Malcolm Feeley, is analogous to these potential civil plaintiffs, in that "the cost of *invoking* one's rights frequently is greater than the loss of the rights themselves." Defendants, whether or not they consider themselves to be innocent, may choose to accept a guilty plea rather than battle against the process.[2] Thus, the determination of guilt or innocence is as irrelevant to the criminal trial as the worth of the claim is to the discrimination case. The worthiness of the discrimination claim is never evaluated when persons who experience discrimination do not transcend the burdens of their victimhood.

The emotional attachment to rights-focused struggles that many Americans share perhaps depends upon the configuration of indigenous group action, moral commitment, and litigation strategies that coexisted during the height of the civil rights movement. Even then, it is not clear that the belief in rights was instrumental in promoting social change. I have put this nostalgia for rights-focused action into perspective by uncovering a pattern of passivity among those who routinely experience injustice and by evaluating the historical events that created the civil rights strategy during the Reconstruction era. The strategy of legal protection was not born of contemporary activism; it has its origins in the immediate aftermath of the Civil War. Thus, the modern conception of civil rights can be seen as a historical accident, one that has created a model for legal reform that has become difficult to repudiate. Yet, contemporary society as the inheritor of this legacy is not powerless against this particular vision of law; it can begin to recreate a language of rights that responds to the struggles and needs of those who experience social and economic disadvantage.

Psychology, Politics, and Social Change

The inaction of victims of discrimination is problematic from the vantage point of the ideology of legal protection. From the social reality of the victim, however, we find that "survival is a form of resistance."[3] The rationality of the response to a legal problem is defined by the situation. To otherwise imply that their standpoint reflects an invalid interpretation of reality denies the fears and hardships in these people's lives. In this study, the majority of these individuals view protest as contrary to their well-being and livelihood. The situation creates a paradox or irrationality, in which people engaged in discrimination conflicts believe they are better off if they decide not to pursue what would seem to be their interests.[4]

The paradox of irrationality is imposed because the few who single themselves out for protest bear the disproportionate burden of the collective struggle. Even if the complainant endures and receives compensation, the psychological and economic consequences of the dispute are likely to be more costly than the benefits of victory. For example, Nora, who pursued a claim, felt she was not fighting to retain her job, for it had already lost its value to her. She was fighting for a principle. John believed he was better off if he submitted to unfair treatment for over a year and secured his job for the long run. To act aggressively and battle for principles requires "irrational" sacrifices. To act in a passive manner appears irrational, yet assures the victim's survival.

Social scientific studies of people engaged in legal disputes typically begin with a model of rational action that assumes that psychological factors are obstacles to the resolution of the problem. The psychological factors influencing the disputant are independent variables in a model that explains why individuals choose among different means of resolving disputes. Conventional approaches often focus on the individual, but diminish the importance of the psychological dimension;

instead, my interpretations are cast from a wider net, one that considers the contingencies that can affect life chances.

My objective is to introduce the reader to the mind of the victim, but not to impose an interpretation that applies categories as they are conventionally used by social scientists or by professionals who "treat" victims. I have avoided this type of categorization because typologies of victims have the insidious effect of characterizing individuals in ways that reinforce negative stereotypes. This study describes the manner of victims—the ways in which victims respond to situations of powerlessness. The psychology of the victim is a reflection of the psychology of the powerful. There is a symmetrical relationship between the powerful and the weak that reflects both the illusions and the realities of their situations.

This view of the psychology of victims is drawn in part from Foucault's conception of ideology and power. Foucault's theories gain substance in the context of his examples, prisons and asylums, where reforms designed to liberate and benefit the excluded are seen as devices for controlling and facilitating a new economy of power. Foucault's account of institutional mechanisms of control gives reason to question strategies of liberation designed by those in power or protecting the interests of the state. My study also owes to Foucault's orientation its message about the uncertain possibilities for social change. Foucault does not speak of struggles against oppression; his analysis is aimed at dismantling the historical understanding of the social world. He illustrates the influence of the powerful on everyday discourse and the manner in which the self is reduced to the "subject" controlled by professions and the state. I offer no new "expert" advice about liberation strategies; but I project a revisionist view that allows subjects to reexamine their fate. While presenting no alternative strategies for liberation, my study formulates a view of the victim's situation unencumbered by standards of objectivity, false responsibility, and legal criteria. This view of the victims' situation appreciates their unique circumstances and courage.

Reconstructing the Civil Rights Society

The conventional view of law provides an unsatisfactory explanation for the failure of antidiscrimination strategies. The neoconservative criticisms of the civil rights strategy, which point out the failure of "group-based" protection and the disproportionate sharing of burdens by minorities and "innocents" within the majority, deny the need for social change. Both the radical and the neoconservative have turned away from law. The radical has rejected legal solutions that justify the

inadequacies of the status quo, and the neoconservative has found governmental intervention both unnecessary and divisive. Even the
liberal's disillusionment with the capacity of the law to promote social
change has furthered a retrenchment on the doctrinal level in school
desegregation and preferential employment practices.

The leaders of the civil rights movement express disillusionment
with progressive strategies in their assessments of the twenty-year civil
rights era, from the passage of the 1964 Civil Rights Act to the mid-1980s.
Coretta Scott King commented on the twentieth anniversary of the
Civil Rights Act:

> Segregationist politicians don't stand at the school house door anymore.
> But segregated housing patterns and more subtle forms of racism prevent
> equal access to a quality public education. . . . All too often "last hired, first
> fired" is still the rule for minorities. . . . Recent Supreme Court decisions
> have shown us how vulnerable affirmative action policies can be when the
> Court's long standing commitment to equality is undermined. It also shows
> how susceptible the. . . [C]ourt is to the winds of political change.[5]

King sees only modest progress during the era for two reasons. First, the
dramatic victories of the sixties are vulnerable to the tide of political
conservatism. Second and more relevant to this analysis is the feeling
that the civil rights movement had the unfortunate consequence of
creating more subtle forms of racism. There is also a growing sentiment
that the civil rights movement has brought about an erosion in the
confidence of minorities. Survey data on political alienation indicate
that in the early 1980s 77 percent of blacks reported feelings of alienation and powerlessness as compared to 33 percent in 1966. The conventional view of antidiscrimination policy might attribute this phenomenon
to cynicism resulting from racial groups' increased awareness of discrimination and circumvention of the law. But this study suggests that
more than twenty years of civil rights "progress" may in fact have contributed to the alienation of excluded groups.

The civil rights movement has produced numerous lessons about
the limits of the law. Blacks, women, and those allied for social progress
have cast doubt on the efficacy of legal reform; however, their questions
have led to even more serious reservations about the desirability of legal
strategies. Champions of litigation may misrepresent the problem, by
ignoring the complexity of systematic processes of discrimination that
operate throughout society, and then misrepresent the solution, by
creating the impression that the elimination of legal barriers is sufficient to achieve racial equality. Litigation thus becomes the focal point
of activism at the cost of possibly more dynamic attacks on the root
causes of racial and sexual subordination.[6] Moreover, legal ideologies

can constrain the social vision of the victim and promote self-blame. The mythologies that perpetuate racism and sexism are reflected both in the benevolent policies of legal reformers and in the self-image of those who experience discrimination.

Progressive scholars have addressed the problems of antidiscrimination policy by attempting to reconcile the historical logic of the law with the need for social change. The antidiscrimination principle embodies a very limited conception of equality, thus creating structural limitations on its application.[7] The norms of judicial decision making accentuate antidiscrimination law's narrow focus on objectivity and individualism.[8] The antidiscrimination principle strives toward objectivity in its application by almost making the "predicate of intervention appear technocratic."[9]

This illusion of judicial neutrality, however, is employed to enhance the legitimacy of judicial policies that set arbitrary limits on when it is appropriate for the courts to intervene. The apparent objectivity of the judicial method is at odds with the more relative conception of injustice among people who experience discrimination. Individuals who are engaged in conflicts are incapable of autonomous action when they depend upon authoritative definitions of objectivity and thus often decide prematurely that their contributory actions invalidate their claim or that they lack sufficient grounds.

The result of these attempts by the interpreters of the law to make antidiscrimination doctrine appear consistent with liberal theory is the failure to promote a belief in rights that will empower persons individually or collectively. First, the cultural predisposition to believe that social failure and success reflect individual responsibility or blame overrules the perception of class-based injustices. In fact, the perception that there are narrowly defined guidelines for a legally recognizable claim encourages individuals to accept their fate rather than take legal recourse. Second, the potential for collective action is diminished because antidiscrimination law does not give meaningful recognition to group-based identities.

The source of these two problems is the meaning of "individuality" in the interpretation of the antidiscrimination principle. Persons making discrimination claims are only in a sense part of a class; their claims are not dependent upon the desires or interests of those similarly situated. The concept of right as employed in the interpretation of the antidiscrimination principle is individualized, yet the idea of right is also universalized. As is explicitly stated in the *Bakke* case, the equal protection clause is designed to protect the rights of *all persons*, not the interests of historically disadvantaged groups. The universalization of rights, in effect, makes the invocation of rights meaningless if the victims cannot state their claims in terms of the treatment of a disadvantaged class of which they consider themselves a member.

Thus, we need to begin the search for a restatement of rights that abandons the objectivity and individuality of current doctrine and that recognizes the interests of social groups and individuals. People who possess salient group identities need to find in the law reinforcement for the expression of their individual selves and positive referents for the qualities they share as a collectivity.

Victims without a Cause

The universalization of individual rights has the ultimate result of rendering important events meaningless. Victims often come away from situations in which they perceive prejudicial treatment feeling isolated and broken. Their anger, emotions, and outrage are dissolved by a sense of confusion and fear. People cannot begin to see their grievances as part of a collective struggle unless they can make sense out of the complex social processes that produce their disadvantaged position in society. The result is that victims of discrimination, whether they use legal channels or not, may never feel redeemed. In my interviews, the individuals' motivations for open disclosure about themselves and their experiences demonstrated their need to overcome the isolation imposed by these experiences: individuals who were "immobilized before the law" saw the interview as an opportunity to give social importance to their painful experiences (e.g., Laura), and persons who paid the costs of exercising their rights and used lawyers wanted to advise others about the inevitable pitfalls and traps encountered by a claimant of discrimination (e.g., Nora).

The reactions of these individuals toward the law confirm Kafka's image of legality: Law, which is both universal and powerless, is incompatible with everyday life. Perhaps the image of the Kafkaesque world is denied or made to appear trivial because it is so compelling and disturbing an explanation for the failure of legal action. The model of legal protection assumes that law transforms people's lives and experiences and that law is meaningfully expressed in the context of their lives. We may find it both intuitively plausible and disconcerting that people see law as a hostile presence in their everyday lives and fear law's destructive potential.

What do the findings suggest about the continuing role of antidiscrimination law in American society? The present era of complacency may permit inequalities linked to race, sex, and other forms of discrimination to continue at historically improved but still intolerable levels. The current political climate is not conducive to the politicization of minorities and the mass political mobilization of the sixties is at risk of becoming a legend. Unfortunately, the activist legend reinforces complacency by reminding society that reform is not always synonymous with failure.

We are currently experiencing, however, a proliferation of antidiscrimination strategies. Such proliferation can be seen as the logical extension of the universalization of rights—by including *all* groups, it further dilutes the benefits received by the historically most disadvantaged groups. From the vantage point of this study, it is not surprising that the universalization of rights has led to increasing tensions between racial, ethnic, and feminist groups. Spokespersons for black interests, who fear that proliferation of rights will dissolve their minimal gains, have begun to object to civil rights strategies that fail to give priority to disadvantaged blacks.

Though antidiscrimination law may have produced positive social change, legal strategies put unacceptable burdens on disadvantaged people with little promise of success. The gap between the symbolic life of the law and the ineffectiveness of the law in action imposes a cost borne by the intended beneficiaries of civil rights policies. The inability of civil rights strategies to fulfill their promise appears to have left many who experience discrimination on uncertain ground between public and private action where they are without faith in themselves or the law.

Appendix A / List of Interviewees*

Betty is a Hispanic woman in her twenties who lives with her family. She experienced racial discrimination while employed in the personnel department of a large corporation (one of the major employers in the city) and was eventually fired from her job after continued harassment by her supervisor.

Carmen is a Hispanic woman who has four children, including a new baby. She lives in a lower-middle-class suburban neighborhood. She experienced sex discrimination in employment, in a situation in which an increase in job responsibilities was not followed by a pay increase.

Carol is a white woman in her twenties who lives in a lower-middle-class integrated neighborhood with her husband. She was denied a job working with mentally handicapped children on the basis of her sex.

Clara is a white woman in her twenties. She rents an apartment in a middle-class suburban neighborhood and works as a white-collar sales professional. She complained of sex discrimination after she discovered that she received a lower salary than other managers.

Deborah is a young white woman who lives in a working-class neighborhood. She has been employed as a truck driver and she complained of sexual harassment by a fellow employee. The situation has remained the same since her complaint to her supervisor; she is at a stand-off with the perpetrator.

Delma is a white woman in her early thirties. She has experienced two incidents of sex discrimination: firing from a car rental agency and sexual harassment on her current job.

Dolores is a black woman in her late thirties who lives in a segregated neighborhood outside a major metropolitan area with her mother and daughter. She experienced discrimination in attempting to secure rental housing and as a welfare recipient.

Helen is a white woman in her seventies who rents an apartment in a "desirable" white neighborhood. She was denied a job in a department store on the basis of her age.

John is black man in his forties who lives with his young daughter. He works as a truck driver and he experienced racial harassment on the job.

Laura is a young black woman who lives with two small chidren in a lower-middle-class black neighborhood in a large metropolitan area. She experienced racial discrimination in employment and sex discrimination in housing.

*The descriptions of the respondents here and in the text have been reported in a manner that protects their anonymity. Therefore it was necessary to exclude identifying information, including full names (and to provide pseudonyms for first names, as appropriate), specific information about the location of their residence, and detailed information about the perpetrator of the act of discrimination.

Martha is an elderly white woman who owns a house in a suburban neighborhood. She complained of sex discrimination in obtaining credit. The incident occurred when she attempted to reestablish her credit after the death of her husband.

Nora is a white woman in her thirties who lives in an apartment in a scenic upper-class neighborhood. She works in a top managerial position in a high-tech industry. She experienced sex discrimination in employment.

Patricia is a black woman in her thirties who experienced racial discrimination in employment and "single parent" discrimination in housing. She lives in a black inner-city neighborhood and shares custody of a teenage son with his father, who lives in another city.

Rachel is a lawyer in her twenties who experienced sex discrimination in employment. While still in law school she was turned down for a job in the legal field on the basis of sex. She now works for the government.

Richard is a black doctor in his fifties. He complained of racial discrimination by the police, who disrupted his medical practice in an inner-city neighborhood.

Sam is an American Indian man who rents an apartment in a lower-class neighborhood. He complained of reverse discrimination in employment, after an incident in which he believes blacks were given preference for a job he pursued.

Sylvia is a young Hispanic woman who lives in a densely populated poor neighborhood. She has had steady employment throughout her adult life. She lives in a one-room apartment with her husband, who recently immigrated from Mexico.

Virginia is a white woman in her thirties who rents an apartment in an urban neighborhood. She experienced sex discrimination while working in a financial management firm.

Appendix B / Interview Schedule

1. Describe the situation which led up to the incident, what occurred, and the outcome of the incident.

2. What other incidents of discrimination have you confronted in your life? Describe these incidents also.

3. How did you know the treatment was due to discrimination?

4. Why did you or did you not complain? Why did you not make demands on the other party?

5. In retrospect, what would you have done differently? What choices do you think you had? What were the constraints on making these choices? What issues were you most concerned with?

6. What costs or harms did you experience because of discrimination? What would you give up to prove you were treated unjustly?

7. What type of issues were you most concerned with (principle?—proving that you are right; or avoiding future conflict?—getting the present problem over with)?

8. Do you feel you acted exceptionally—did you have any unusual insight or make any extra effort? Did you act differently than other people you know would act in this situation?

9. Do you think this happens to other people like you? How often and in what kind of situations?

10. Who were the people you talked to about the problem? What did they suggest you do? Did they agree or disagree with your original interpretation? How influential were they?

11. Did you use any governmental agency, community organization, professional service, etc., to help you deal with the problem?

12. Who was your opponent? What did he or she act like? What do you think were their interests? Do you feel they think they were acting justly? What do you think are the motives of most people who perpetuate discrimination?

13. How would you make a legal case out of the situation? What would the law defend? Who would be the parties? What would be the claim? What outcome would make you satisfied?

14. What was your emotional state during the conflict—excited, angry, frustrated, frightened, depressed?

15. Do you think anyone thought less of you because of the incident of discrimination?

16. Do you feel the incident caused disruption in your life? How much?

17. Did you think you were not being evaluated as an individual? Were you labeled and not looked at for what you are? How did they make you feel?

18. What do you think is your responsibility to prevent your own harm or defend yourself in situations of discrimination?

19. Could you have done anything to prevent the incident from occurring? Do you do anything now to avoid being discriminated against?

20. Who is responsible for what happened to you?

21. Do you think most people would support your interests? Would most people feel you had been mistreated? What "other people" are you thinking about?

22. Is the law on your side? Should the law be on your side?

23. Does discrimination law treat race, age, and gender claims similarly? What kind of remedies do you think the law provides?

24. In general, do you think some people get special treatment by the law?

25. On what characteristics do you think it is fair to evaluate other people? What justifies some people making more money than others?

26. Compare yourself with other people you have known. Do you feel you have accomplished a lot? Do others deserve what they got? Why are some people richer or poorer, more or less successful?

27. Do you feel you deserve a better job? Better housing, education, other things?

28. Has government made your life better or worse? Should the government have done anything to help you in this discrimination experience?

29. What would an ideal society be like? How much equality, freedom, privacy, togetherness, peacefulness, diversity?

30. Do people in power in government understand the problems of people like you?

31. Are you satisified with your social position?

32. What things really matter in your life? What do you value most? What are your primary goals?

33. How important are you to your job, family, friends?

34. What are the important constraints on your life? What have been the major turning points in your life? What setbacks have you experienced? How did you react to them?

35. What are your best and worst qualities?

36. What other situations make you angry or feel you have been treated unjustly? How do you react in these situations?

37. Do people you know really well treat you differently than strangers do?

38. Can one person do much to change things?

39. What political activities have you been involved in? What organized groups do you belong to?

40. In this particular situation, what would make you feel redeemed? What would make you feel justice has been done? What did you want, or what would have made you happier?

Notes

One / *The Model of Legal Protection*

1. For a longitudinal study of the effects of civil rights reforms on black and white incomes, see Donald J. McCrone and Richard J. Hardy, "Civil Rights and the Achievement of Racial Economic Equality, 1948–1975," *American Journal of Political Science* 22 (1978):1–17.

2. Morroe Berger, *Equality by Statute* (New York: Doubleday, 1967), 5.

3. Gunnar Myrdal, *An American Dilemma: The Negro Problem and Modern Democracy* (New York: McGraw-Hill, 1944), ixx.

4. Ibid., lxxi. Tocqueville also was struck by the tension between freedom and equalitarianism in American society: see *Democracy in America*, ed. Francis Bowen (New York: Knopf, 1965).

5. Myrdal, *American Dilemma*, lxxii. Another important book that takes on the same viewpoint of combating prejudice through moral education is Gordon Allport's *The Nature of Prejudice* (Boston: Beacon Press, 1954). Allport is responding to the emergence of social intolerance of racial and religious groups during World War II.

6. Myrdal, *American Dilemma*, lxxvi.

7. There is academic debate over the original interpretation of the Fourteenth Amendment: see for example, William Winslow Crosskey, *Politics and the Constitution in the History of the United States* (Chicago: University of Chicago Press, 1951); Raoul Berger, *Government by Judiciary: The Transformation of the Fourteenth Amendment* (Cambridge: Harvard University Press, 1977); Jacobus tenBroek, *Equal under Law* (London: Collier, 1965); and Robert M. Cover, *Justice Accused: Anti-Slavery and the Judicial Process* (New Haven: Yale University Press, 1975).

8. The state action doctrine is a judicial self-limitation on the reach of governmental control over private entities. In *The Civil Rights Cases*, 109 U.S. 3 (1883), the Court invalidated the public accommodations provision of the 1875 Civil Rights Act. This decision held that "state action," the prohibition of state conduct, was necessary to establish a violation of the Fourteenth Amendment. The subsequent interpretations of state action in civil rights cases have reinforced the underlying principle that the deprivation of freedom and liberties is the consequence of excessive governmental power and that the appropriateness of governmental behavior is determined through an evaluation of its neutrality. See, for example, *Shelley v. Kraemer*, 334 U.S. 1 (1948), and *Burton v. Wilmington Parking Authority*, 365 U.S. 715 (1961).

9. 407 U.S. 163 (1972).

10. As the model of legal protection is made explicit, the question arises: what legitimates this view of antidiscrimination law? Policies of protection are

often treated with suspicion; they are seen as euphemisms for control over minorities and other groups. Policies of law and legislation protecting children, drinkers, women, delinquents, and others have historically lost their reputations as benign social reforms. See, for example, the fate of the legal movements discussed in Andrew T. Scull, *Decarceration: Community Treatment and the Deviant—A Radical View* (Englewood Cliffs, N.J.: Prentice-Hall, 1977), and Anthony Platt, *The Child Savers: The Invention of Delinquency* (Chicago: University of Chicago Press, 1977). Why does the protectionism of antidiscrimination law remain less overt and more deeply rooted in a strategy of social change? Part of the answer is that antidiscrimination law is a form of protectionism which is consistent with the role of limited government. To the extent that antidiscrimination policies are a response to unnecessary or adverse restrictions of government, protectionism supports actions inhibiting governmental intervention.

11. 42 U.S.C. § 2000-2(a).

12. Civil Rights Act of 1964. See also *McDonnell Douglas Corp. v. Green*, 411 U.S. 792 (1973).

13. 401 U.S. 424 (1971). The Court ruled that testing and measuring devices must demonstrate "a reasonable measure of job performance."

14. Plaintiffs utilize "disparate impact" analysis (based upon statistical data) in an attempt to establish a prima facie case. See, for example, *Hazelwood School District v. United States*, 433 U.S. 299 (1977).

15. *Delaware State College v. Ricks*, 101 S. Ct. 498 (1980). This case requires that the defendant receive notification from the EEOC within ten days of the possibility of suit and that the suit be brought within 180 days, or in some cases 300 days.

16. *Robinson v. Lorillard Corp.*, 444 F.2d 791 (4th Cir. 1971).

17. 383 F. Supp. 1157 (N.D. Ala. 1974).

18. *Franks v. Bowman Transportation Co.*, 424 U.S. 747 (1976).

19. There are also important differences in antidiscrimination strategies in relation to race, sex, and other social groupings, and there is a complex set of doctrines relating to state action, school desegregation, voting rights, and other racial and sexual categorizations in litigation.

20. See, for example, Ruth G. Blumrosen, "Wage Discrimination, Job Segregation, and Title VII of the Civil Rights Act of 1964," *University of Michigan Journal of Law Reform* 12 (1979):397–502; also Nadine Taub, "Keeping Women in Their Place: Stereotyping Per Se as a Form of Employment Discrimination," *Boston College Law Review* 21 (1980):345–418.

21. For example, *South Carolina v. Katzenbach*, 383 U.S. 301 (1966); *Jones v. Mayer*, 392 U.S. 409 (1968).

22. Alan Freeman, "Legitimizing Discrimination through Anti-Discrimination Law: A Critical Review of Supreme Court Doctrine," *Minnesota Law Review* 62 (1978):1049–1119.

23. For a discussion of the appropriate forms of disputes suitable for litigation, see Lon Fuller, "The Forms and Limits of Adjudication," *Harvard Law Review* 92 (1978):353–409.

24. See Catharine MacKinnon, *Sexual Harassment of Working Women: A Case of Sex Discrimination* (New Haven: Yale University Press, 1979).

25. This has been described as the "individualist bias" of antidiscrimination policies: see Kathryn L. Powers, "Sex Segregation and the Ambivalent Directions of Sex Discrimination Law," *Wisconsin Law Review,* 1979, no. 1:55–124.

26. Alan Goldman, *Justice and Reverse Discrimination* (Princeton: Princeton University Press, 1979), 73.

27. This model of law is developed in Donald Black, "The Mobilization of the Law," *Journal of Legal Studies* 2 (1973):125–49. Black's model refers to the mobilization of law in general, not specifically to antidiscrimination law.

28. Ibid., 127.

29. Ibid., 146.

30. Howard Zinn, "The Conspiracy of Law," in *The Rule of Law,* ed. Robert Paul Wolff (New York: Simon & Schuster, 1971), 15–36.

31. *Green v. County School Board,* 391 U.S. 430 (1968).

32. For the history of the Court and school desegregation, see Raymond Wolters, *The Burden of Brown: Thirty Years of School Desegregation* (Knoxville: University of Tennessee Press, 1984); J. Harvie Wilkinson III, ed., *From Brown to Bakke: The Supreme Court and School Integration, 1954–1978* (New York: Oxford University Press, 1979).

33. See, for example, Herbert Wechsler, "Toward Neutral Principles of Constitutional Law," *Harvard Law Review* 73 (1959):1–35.

34. John Hart Ely, *Democracy and Distrust: A Theory of Judicial Review* (Cambridge: Harvard University Press, 1980), 43–72.

35. For a critique of process theories of judicial review, see Laurence H. Tribe, "The Puzzling Persistence of Process-based Constitutional Theories," *Yale Law Journal* 89 (1981):1063–80.

36. Ely, *Democracy and Distrust,* 148–69.

37. Roberto Unger, *The Critical Legal Studies Movement* (Cambridge: Harvard University Press, 1986), 49.

38. Donald Horowitz, *The Courts and Social Policy* (Washington, D.C.: Brookings Institution, 1977); Abram Chayes, "The Role of the Judge in Public Law Litigation," *Harvard Law Review* 89 (1976):1281–1316.

39. Owen M. Fiss, "Groups and the Equal Protection Clause," in *Equality and Preferential Treatment,* ed. Marshall Cohen, Thomas Nagel, and Thomas Scanlon (Princeton: Princeton University Press, 1977), 103.

40. Nathan Glazer, *Affirmative Discrimination: Ethnic Inequality and Public Policy* (New York: Basic Books, 1978), 30.

41. Ibid., 58.

42. Ibid., 75.

43. Fiss, "Groups and the Equal Protection Clause," 134.

44. Unger, *The Critical Legal Studies Movement,* 36.

45. Thomas Sowell, *Civil Rights: Rhetoric or Reality?* (New York: Morrow, 1984), 17.

46. Ibid., 57–59.

47. Ibid., 24–28.

48. Ibid., 168–95.

49. Gary S. Becker, *The Economics of Discrimination* (Chicago: University of Chicago Press, 1957).

50. Glen C. Loury, "A Dynamic Theory of Racial Income Differences," in *Women, Minorities, and Employment Discrimination,* ed. Phyllis A. Wallace and Annette M. LaMond (Lexington, Mass.: Lexington Books, 1977).

51. See Elisabeth M. Almquist, "Women in the Labor Force," *Signs* 2 (1977): 843–55; Isabell Sawhill, "Discrimination and Poverty among Women Who Head Families," *Signs* 1 (1976): 201–11; Marianne A. Ferber and Helen M. Lowry, "Women: The New Reserve Army of the Unemployed," *Signs* 1 (1976): 213–32.

52. Hannah Arendt, "Reflections on Little Rock," *Dissent* 6 (Winter 1959): 45–56.

53. Ibid., 8.

54. Elisabeth Young-Bruehl, *Hannah Arendt: For the Love of the World* (New Haven: Yale University Press, 1982), 308–18; Hannah Arendt, *Rahel Varnhagen: The Life of a Jewish Woman* (New York: Harcourt Brace Jovanovich, 1974).

55. Hannah Arendt, *The Human Condition* (Chicago: University of Chicago Press, 1958).

56. Arendt, *Reflections,* 51.

57. Ibid., 50.

58. Quoted in Young-Bruehl, *Hannah Arendt,* 316. The quotation is from Robert Penn Warren, ed., *Who Speaks for the Negro?* (New York: Random House, 1965), 342–44.

59. Stokely Carmichael and Charles V. Hamilton, *Black Power: The Politics of Liberation in America* (New York: Vintage Books, 1967).

60. Robert L. Scott and Wayne Brockriede, eds., *The Rhetoric of Black Power* (New York: Harper & Row, 1969), 25–64.

61. James Boggs, *Racism and the Class Struggle: Further Pages from a Black Worker's Notebook* (New York: Monthly Review Press, 1970), 100.

62. Ibid., 81–91.

63. Claybourne Carson, *In Struggle: SNCC and the Black Awakening of the 1960s* (Cambridge: Harvard University Press, 1981), 215–304.

64. Stuart Scheingold, *The Politics of Rights* (New Haven: Yale University Press, 1974), 130.

65. Ibid., 100–107; Harrell R. Rodgers, Jr., and Charles S. Bullock III, *Law and Social Change: Civil Rights Laws and Their Consequences* (New York: McGraw-Hill, 1972); Owen M. Fiss, "School Desegregation: The Uncertain Path of the Law," in *Equality and Preferential Treatment,* ed. Marshall Cohen, Thomas Nagel, and Thomas Scanlon (Princeton: Princeton University Press, 1977), 155–91.

66. Scheingold, *The Politics of Rights,* 144.

67. For an account that suggests the limitation in the "individualizing" logic of the Court, see Fiss, "Groups and the Equal Protection Clause," 84–154;

for another disenchanted liberal position that focuses on bureaucratic contingencies, see Joel Handler, *Social Movements and the Legal System* (New York: Academic Press, 1978).

68. Derrick Bell, "Foreword: The Civil Rights Chronicles," *Harvard Law Review* 98 (November 1985): 8.

69. Ibid., 8n.

70. Alan D. Freeman, "Anti-Discrimination Law: A Critical Review," in *The Politics of Law: A Progressive Critique*, ed. David Kairys (New York: Pantheon Books, 1982), 96–116.

71. The legal system has a significant discriminatory impact through routine case processing in criminal courts. Conflict criminologists have documented the ways in which race is an illegitimate influence on decisions to arrest, prosecute, and sentence minorities in criminal courts. The evidence of discriminatory outcomes of criminal court decision making leads some criminologists to conclude that courts are institutions of domination, engaged in the control of rebellious minority group behavior. For a review of the sentencing literature, see John Hagen and Kristin Bumiller, "Making Sense of Sentencing," in *Research on Sentencing: The Search for Reform*, ed. Alfred Blumstein (Washington, D.C.: National Academy Press, 1983), 2:1–54. See also Richard Quinney, *Class, State, and Crime*, 2d ed. (New York: Longman, 1980), and Ian Taylor, Paul Walton, and Jock Young, *The New Criminology: For a Social Theory of Deviance* (New York: Harper & Row, 1973).

72. The repressive function of the courts is expanded during times of crisis, when the political elite attempts to "criminalize" violent protest. Because during the 1960s black leaders and most of their following accepted a nonviolent, integrationist stance, ghetto revolts were "occasions for embarrassment" to the civil rights movement as a whole: "The commitment to nonviolence...mitigated against the capacity and inclination of black political leaders to oppose the court authority's definition of the situation [the ghetto riots] as ordinary crime." The emphasis on the formal achievement of "equal rights" directed black leaders' concerns to the short-run risk of severe criminal sanctions for the rioters. The leaders, thus preoccupied with "formal justice," ignored the long-run interests of blacks as an exploited class. The radical strategist claims that concern for formal equality in effect legitimizes the repressive functions of the courts. See Isaac D. Balbus, *The Dialectics of Legal Repression: Black Rebels before the American Criminal Courts* (New York: Russell Sage Foundation, 1973), 258.

73. W. Hayward Burns, "Race Discrimination Law and Race in America," in *The Politics of Law: A Progressive Critique*, ed. David Kairys (New York: Pantheon Books, 1982), 89–95.

74. Freeman, "Legitimizing Discrimination," 1049–1119.

75. For a sympathetic critique of critical legal scholars' work on antidiscrimination law and a discussion of the desirability of rights discourse, see Kimberle Crenshaw, "Race, Reform, and Retrenchment: Transformation and Legitimation in Antidiscrimination Law," *Harvard Law Review* 101, forthcoming, December 1987.

76. See, for example, Martha L. Fineman, "Implementing Equality: Ideology, Contradiction, and Social Change. A Study of Rhetoric and Result in the Regulation of the Consequences of Divorce," *Wisconsin Law Review*, 1983, no. 4:789–886.

77. Isabel Marcus et al., "Feminist Discourse, Moral Values, and the Law—A Conversation," *Buffalo Law Review* 34 (1985):11–87.

78. Carol Gilligan, *In a Different Voice: Psychological Theory and Women's Development* (Cambridge: Harvard University Press, 1982).

79. Julia Brophy and Carol Smart, eds., *Women in Law* (London: Routledge & Kegan Paul, 1985), 17.

80. Bell, "Civil Rights Chronicles," 36.

Two / Law and Ideology

1. See Duncan Kennedy, "Toward an Historical Understanding of Legal Consciousness: The Case of Classical Legal Thought in America, 1850–1940," *Research in Law and Sociology* 3 (1980):3–24.

2. Philippe Nonet and Philip Selznick, *Law and Society in Transition* (New York: Harper & Row, 1978).

3. Lon Fuller, "American Legal Realism," *University of Pennsylvania Law Review* 82 (1934):443 (emphasis added). Fuller goes on to be critical of "left-wing" realism.

4. Jerome Frank, *Law and the Modern Mind* (New York: Brentano's, 1930), 217–21.

5. Leon Mayhew, *Law and Equal Opportunity: A Study of the Massachusetts Commission against Discrimination* (Cambridge: Harvard University Press, 1968), 232–34.

6. Patricia Ward Crowe, "Complainant Reactions to the Massachusetts Commission against Discrimination," *Law and Society Review* 12 (1978): 217–35.

7. Ibid., 233.

8. Joel Handler, *Social Movements and the Legal System* (New York: Academic Press, 1978).

9. An exception to this conclusion is a recent empirical study that concludes that the EEO has had substantial success in the enforcement of discrimination claims. This conclusion is based, however, on a definition of success at the highest level (in court) and for more advantaged groups. The study found it "desirable" that the majority of EEO cases involved "class action, upper level jobs, [and] supervisory jobs" because the "decisions have the potential to affect many members of the protected groups and to improve their access to all kinds of jobs." (Thus, they assume that a "trickle–down" effect benefits the most disadvantaged groups.) Paul Burstein and Kathleen Monaghan, "Equal Employment Opportunity and the Mobilization of Law," *Law and Society Review* 20 (1986):368. This study, rather than discovering success, may be evidence of commissions' propensity to invest their energies in the few best claims and expending few resources on cases that would be difficult to

substantiate, a pattern similar to the one found by Leon Mayhew in his pioneering study of the implementation of antidiscrimination law.

10. The initial survey was conducted by the Civil Litigation Research Project by telephone in five federal judicial districts: South Carolina, Eastern Pennsylvania, Eastern Wisconsin, New Mexico, and Central California. The districts were chosen to maximize geographical and demographic diversity. The respondents were asked whether anyone in their household had experienced one or more of a list of problems in the past three years. If the respondents indicated they had experienced a discrimination problem, they were administered an additional "problem" questionnaire with forty-four closed-ended and open-ended questions. The data reported in table 1 are derived from open-ended questions included in the survey which were previously uncoded. The methodology is described in Herbert M. Kritzer, "Studying Disputes: Learning from the CLRP Experience," *Law and Society Review* 15 (1980–81):503–24.

11. Richard E. Miller and Austin Sarat, "Grievances, Claims, and Disputes: Assessing the Adversary Culture," *Law and Society Review* 15 (1980–81):525–66.

12. Attribution theory attempts to explain why individuals blame themselves for the dispute (i.e., the need to maintain perceived control); however, this provides a limited psychological explanation for behavior and does not raise questions about the consequences of self-defeat. See Dan Coates and Steven Penrod, "Social Psychology and the Emergence of Disputes," *Law and Society Review* 15 (1980–81):655–80. For an interpretation similar to my own, see Sally Merry and Susan S. Silbey, "What Do Plaintiffs Want? Re-examining the Concept of Dispute," *Justice System Journal* 9 (1984):151–78.

13. This function of justice is expressed effectively in Simone de Beauvoir, *The Ethics of Ambiguity* (Secaucus, N.J.: Citadel Press, 1980).

14. The interviews were guided by forty questions on the following topics: (1) the circumstances of the discrimination incident; (2) the relationship of the incident to other acts of discrimination or other forms of perceived mistreatment; (3) justifications for the respondents' actions in response to the incident; (4) their feelings about fairness, competition, merit, and status inequalities; (5) their attitudes about their own self-worth and competence; (6) their political mind: degree of trust in government, political alienation and cynicism, extent of political participation, and attitudes toward leaders and authority; (7) their knowledge of the political and legal process and their interpretation of antidiscrimination law; (8) the consequences of the actions they took in response to the discrimination problem and their evaluations, in retrospect, of how their strategies in the conflict situation were modified over time; (9) their beliefs about the effectiveness of political and legal action.

15. The intensive interviewing was conducted in two judicial districts: Eastern Wisconsin (Milwaukee metropolitan area) and Central California (Los Angeles County) (their selection was dependent upon the geographical constraints on the investigator; however, variation by locality was not relevant to the objectives of the intensive interviewing). Interviews were attempted with all respondents experiencing discrimination problems in the two districts.

Cases were eliminated if they had refused to provide their name, address, and phone number and if their description of the problem was inappropriate.

16. The prototype of this method of research in political science is Robert Lane, *Political Ideology* (New York: Free Press, 1962). A recent study of similar design is Jennifer Hochschild, *What's Fair? American Beliefs about Distributive Justice* (Cambridge: Harvard University Press, 1981).

17. For characteristics of the interviewees, see Appendix A. Their characteristics correspond fairly closely to the overall sample, in which there were, by type of problem: 56% employment, 12% education, 18% housing, 14% other; and type of discrimination: 13% age, 22% sex, 31% race, and 34% other. There were a disproportionate number of women in the intensive interview sample because they had a higher response rate.

18. Karl Mannheim, *Ideology and Utopia: An Introduction to the Sociology of Knowledge* (New York: Harcourt, Brace, 1936), 13.

19. Ibid., 40.

20. Ibid., 76.

21. The instrumental Marxist perspective on mass consciousness, that it is a reflection of "global" ideology or "false consciousness," is particularly unsatisfying for the empirical study of the law in action. Critical inquiries of law as a means of social control have often imposed the metaphor of "reflection" to account for the interrelationship between the legal realm and the social and economic sphere. The focus of critical analysis is the legal form (doctrine, regulations, procedures, adversary forums, etc.), which masks the legitimating functions of the law. The primary agent of social control is legal doctrine, which mirrors the policies of economic domination or structural contradictions of the liberal state. Even when presented with great complexity, the consciousness of the "legal subject" is seen as a reflection of legal doctrine, implying that there is an underlying truth that cannot be uncovered by empirical investigation.

Anthropological studies of law and culture resist this tendency. In anthropologists' observations of law and society, ideology stems from, and becomes incorporated into, social practices. From their perspective, law is a filtering mechanism that transmits categories of thought and forms of discourse which influence the understanding of social problems and life situations. The understanding of ideology as metaphor makes sense of the social world; however, it does not focus the inquiry on the nature of power relations and social control. A recent article by Alan Hunt summarizes the difficulties in formulating an adequate understanding of ideology and law: see "The Ideology of Law: Advances and Problems in Recent Applications of the Concept of Ideology to the Analysis of Law," *Law and Society Review* 19 (1985):11–37. For an example of the anthropological understanding of ideology and its application to a study of working-class consciousness, see Sally Merry, "Concepts of Law and Justice among Working Class Americans: Ideology as Culture," *Legal Studies Forum* 9 (1985):59–70.

22. Max Weber, *Economy and Society*, ed. Guenther Roth and Claus Wittich (Berkeley and Los Angeles: University of California Press, 1968), 2:894.

23. Georg Lukács, *History and Class Consciousness: Studies in Marxist Dialectics* (Cambridge: MIT Press, 1968), 97.

24. Herbert Marcuse, *One-Dimensional Man* (Boston: Beacon Press, 1964), 6.

25. Michel Foucault, *Power/Knowledge* (New York: Pantheon Books, 1980).

26. Michel Foucault, *Discipline and Punish: The Birth of the Prison* (New York: Vintage Books, 1979), 20–21.

27. Ibid., 272.

28. Foucault, *Power/Knowledge*, 37. The conception of positive functions of state power does not originate with Foucault. See Claus Offe, "Structural Problems of the Capitalist State," *German Political Studies* 1 (1974):31–56, and Nicos Poulantzas, *State, Power, and Socialism* (London: NLB, 1978).

29. Foucault, *Power/Knowledge*, 102.

30. The most striking impression of the interviewees is the seriousness with which they viewed their roles as providers of information. It was my impression that they responded to questions in an honest and frank fashion. They also made obvious how valuable it is for them to talk about incidents that happened long in the past and to engage in discussions with a high intensity of feeling.

31. Abraham Blumberg, "The Practice of Law as a Confidence Game: The Organizational Cooptation of a Profession," *Law and Society Review* 1 (1967): 15–39; William Simon, "The Ideology of Advocacy: Procedural Justice and Professional Ethics," *Wisconsin Law Review*, 1978, no. 1:29–144.

32. The conventional guidelines for social science interviewing stress the importance of objectivity, precision, order, and conceptualization: see John Lofland, *Analyzing Social Settings* (Belmont, Calif.: Wadsworth, 1971), 1–8, 13, 24. In intensive interviewing, as opposed to structured interviewing, researchers are engaged in a process of discovery. The interviewers elicit responses without imposing their own preconceived categories.

Investigators analyze their own reactions, usually recorded in a field research journal, with the purpose of assuring objectivity. Their field notes inform them how their outlook is being modified by their personal experiences as quasi-subjects in a new environment. The concern is that the experiences do not contaminate the study rather than stressing the ambiguity of the social scientific role in relation to the subject.

The role of the researcher in the field is thus defined by the methodological focus of qualitative research. As a qualitative research method guide explains, quantitative analysis is interested in "causes" and "consequences" of the social phenomenon, while qualitative analysis asks, "What are the characteristics of the social phenomenon, the form it assumes, the variation it displays?" The analysis of qualitative data thus focuses on typology and the definition of "meaning" among participants in a social world. For this reason, conventional methodology narrows the vision and purpose of qualitative methods.

33. Ralf Dahrendorf, *Life Chances: Approaches to Social and Political Theory* (Chicago: University of Chicago Press, 1979).

34. Ibid., 61.

35. Bruno Bettelheim, *Surviving and Other Essays* (New York: Vintage Books, 1980), 88.

36. Niklas Luhmann, "Communication about Law in Interactional Systems," in *Advances in Social Theory and Methodology: Toward an Integration of Micro- and Macro-Sociology*, ed. K. Knorr-Cetina and A. V. Cicourel (Boston: Routledge & Kegan Paul, 1981), 234–56.

37. Foucault, *Knowledge/Power*, 96.

38. Ibid., 97.

39. For a critique of Foucault on this account, see Boaventura de Sousa Santos, "On Modes of Production of Social Power and Law," Institute for Legal Studies Working Paper, vol. 1, no. 1, Law School, University of Wisconsin—Madison (1985), 45: "While Foucault is correct in positing the existence of power forms outside the state, he goes too far in stressing their dispersion and fragmentation. He is left with no theory of the hierarchy of power forms and consequently with no theory of social transformation."

40. Murray Edelman, "Art as Liberating Political Communication," *Institut fur Hohere Studien Journal* 6 (1982):1–15. My interpretation of the interviews reflects the insights of alternative methodologies—phenomenology, ethnomethodology, and cultural interpretativism. I was influenced by the following discussions of method: Clifford Geertz, "Blurred Genres: The Reconfiguration of Social Thought," Chap. 1 in *Local Knowledge: Further Essays in Interpretive Anthropology* (New York: Basic Books, 1983); Boaventura de Sousa Santos, "Science and Politics: Doing Research in Rio's Squatter Settlements," in *Law and Social Enquiry*, ed. Robin Luchman (Uppsala: Scandinavian Institute of African Studies, 1981); George Psathas, ed., *Everyday Language: Studies in Ethnomethodology* (New York: Wiley, 1979).

41. Herbert Marcuse, *The Aesthetic Dimension* (Boston: Beacon Press, 1977).

42. For example, George Steiner, *Language and Silence: Essays on Language, Literature, and the Inhuman* (New York: Atheneum, 1967), contrasts the scholar in the study with the brutal reality of oppression.

Three / The Historical Roots of Antidiscrimination Ideology

1. The United States Constitution, in fact, recognizes the institution of slavery.

2. Clifford Geertz, *The Interpretation of Cultures* (New York: Basic Books, 1973).

3. Michel Foucault, *Discipline and Punish: The Birth of the Prison* (New York: Vintage Books, 1979). See also Douglas Hay et al., eds., *Albion's Fatal Tree: Crime and Society in Eighteenth-Century England* (New York: Pantheon Books, 1975).

4. An analogy can be drawn to the restructuring of illegalities during the 1830s in France from generalized forms of punishment as public spectacles to the "production of delinquency." Foucault sees this transition in criminal law as a "technical mutation" wherein a new strategy transformed an "undifferen-

tiated, abstract, confused penalty" into a "project of corrective technique" associated with the modern prison (*Discipline and Punish*, 257). The transition contained popular illegalities (banditry, peasant uprisings) by creating an "enclosed illegality" (the prison) that supervises and normalizes the actions of the delinquent. The production of delinquency followed from a "basic legalism" that separated delinquents from a "moralized" lower class (285). Seen in the context of the production of delinquency, the failure of prisons to reform delinquents is a "consequence rather than a contradiction." Foucault suggests, "One would be forced to suppose that the prison, and no doubt punishment in general, is not intended to eliminate offences, but rather to distinguish them, to distribute them . . . to assimilate the transgression of the laws in a general tactics of subjection" (272). The prison's obvious failures, recidivism and the creation of a permanent class of delinquents, serves the purposive function of preventing uncontainable and widely dispersed rebellious activities. The production of delinquency rechannels illegalities in ways that are useful, tolerable, or isolating.

5. Delinquency was "produced" in modern society when criminal law and corrective institutions replaced old forms of control over popular illegalities. The example of the production of delinquency is seen as an adjustment of the power of criminal law to conform to a "more generally accepted consensus concerning the power to punish." Eighteenth-century penal reform produced a new technology to administer illegalities and created techniques ("more widely spread in the social body") that conformed to political and moral conditions (ibid., 82). The transformed structure of power was more efficient both politically and economically than unsupervised illegalities. The production of delinquency also reveals how the process of reform is synonymous with the new technique. Explicitly, the failure of the prison is found in its design; the "prison cannot fail to produce delinquents" (266), and "the proclamation of the failure of the prison has always been accompanied by its maintenance" (272). While the prison serves the purposes of controlling the delinquent, the failure in its stated goals publicizes the need for a continued process of institutional reform.

6. Arthur Bestor, "The American Civil War as a Constitutional Crisis," *American Historical Review* 69 (1964):327–52.

7. Barrington Moore, Jr., *The Social Origins of Dictatorship and Democracy: Lord and Peasant in the Making of the Modern World* (Boston: Beacon Press, 1966), 111–55.

8. Stanley M. Elkins, *Slavery: A Problem in American Institutional and Intellectual Life* (Chicago: University of Chicago Press, 1959), 49–52.

9. Mark Tushnet, *The American Law of Slavery, 1810–1860: Considerations of Humanity and Interest* (Princeton: Princeton University Press, 1981), 116, 155.

10. Elkins, *Slavery*, 34.

11. See also Daniel Boorstin, *The Decline of Radicalism: Reflections on America Today* (New York: Random House, 1969), 82–84.

12. Eugene Genovese, *Roll, Jordan, Roll* (New York: Vintage Books, 1976).

13. Harold Hyman and William M. Wiecek, *Equal Justice under Law: Constitutional Development, 1835–1875* (New York: Harper & Row, 1982), 167.

14. Ibid., 278.

15. John Hope Franklin, *Reconstruction after the Civil War* (Chicago: University of Chicago Press, 1961), 49–50; Hyman and Wiecek, *Equal Justice*, 319.

16. Hyman and Wiecek, *Equal Justice*, 152.

17. Stanley Kutler, *Judicial Power and Reconstruction Politics* (Chicago: University of Chicago Press, 1968), 168; see also Robert M. Cover, "The Origins of Judicial Activism in the Protection of Minorities," *Yale Law Journal* 91 (1982):1287–1316.

18. Stephen J. Riegel, "The Persistent Career of Jim Crow: Lower Federal Courts and the Separate but Equal Doctrine, 1865–1896," *American Journal of Legal History* 28 (1984):17–40; but see also C. Vann Woodward, *The Strange Career of Jim Crow* (New York: Oxford University Press, 1955).

19. Kutler, *Judicial Power*, 167.

20. C. Vann Woodward, "Seeds of Failure in Radical Race Policy," in *New Frontiers of the American Reconstruction*, ed. Harold Hyman (Urbana: University of Illinois Press, 1966).

21. Hyman and Wiecek, *Equal Justice*, 508.

22. Ibid., 509. Emphasis added.

23. Ibid., 510.

24. William Cohen, "Negro Involuntary Servitude in the South, 1865–1940," *Journal of Southern History* 42 (1976):33–34; Pete Daniel, "The Metamorphosis of Slavery, 1865–1900," *Journal of American History* 66 (1978):88–99.

25. Daniel, "Metamorphosis," 90.

26. Cohen, "Involuntary Servitude," passim.

27. Ibid., 330.

28. Hyman and Wiecek, *Equal Justice*, 299.

29. Ibid., 508. These three characteristics are identified by Hyman and Wiecek.

30. The rest of this section draws heavily from Claybourne Carson's and Aldon Morris's works cited below. Recently, these historians have provided a reinterpretation of the civil rights movement that has recognized the indigenous roots of the struggle.

31. Aldon D. Morris, *The Origins of the Civil Rights Movement: Black Communities Organizing for Change* (New York: Free Press, 1984), 15.

32. Quoted in Claybourne Carson, *In Struggle* (Cambridge: Harvard University Press, 1981), 23.

33. Morris, *Origins of the Civil Rights Movement*, 37.

34. Ibid., 35.

35. Ibid., 85.

36. Ibid., 40–76.

37. Carson, *In Struggle*, 299.

38. Morris, *Origins of the Civil Rights Movement*, 289–90.

39. Charles E. Fager, *Selma 1965: The March That Changed the South* (Boston: Beacon Press, 1985).

40. Martin Luther King, Jr., *Stride toward Freedom* (1958), excerpted in Leon Friedman, ed., *The Civil Rights Reader* (New York: Walker, 1968), 33–43.

41. Elkins, *Slavery*, 11.

42. Willie Lee Rose, *Slavery and Freedom* (New York: Oxford University Press, 1982), 20–21.

43. Ibid., 24–25.

44. Elkins, *Slavery*, 23.

Four / The Ideology of the Victim

1. Several respondents were chosen for more detailed descriptions here. For an overview of all respondents, see Appendix A.

2. Otto Kirchheimer, *Political Justice: The Use of Legal Procedure for Political Ends* (Princeton: Princeton University Press, 1961), 225–29.

3. Ibid., 225.

4. Ibid., 228.

5. Ibid., 229.

6. Occasionally the defendant in a discrimination case (e.g., Allan Bakke in 1977 and Christine Craft in 1983) gains public notoriety. But, to use Kirchheimer's reference to the celebrated criminal trial, these personal dimensions are only important "to the extent that they bear on the personal history of the defendant.... Sometimes they are immensely interesting; sometimes they suddenly disclose or expose hidden aspects and dimensions of contemporary civilization. Withal, they are memorable and important as *cases* rather than *causes*." Ibid., 49.

7. This consequence of legality is discussed in Chapter 6 as an analogy to the story about law in Kafka's *The Trial*.

8. Alexis de Tocqueville, *Democracy in America*, ed. Francis Bowen (New York: Knopf, 1956), 1:140.

9. The concept of a "juristic person" as a "technical legal solution" is discussed in Max Weber, *Economy and Society*, ed. Guenther Roth and Claus Wittich (Berkeley and Los Angeles: University of California Press, 1968), 2:705–6.

10. Joseph Vining, *Legal Identity: The Coming of Age of Public Man* (New Haven: Yale University Press, 1978), 181.

11. *Duke Power Co. v. Carolina Environmental Study Group*, 437 U.S. 937 (1978); *Heights v. Metropolitan Housing Development Corporation*, 429 U.S. 252 (1977); *Worth v. Seldin*, 422 U.S. 490 (1975); *Sierra Club v. Morton*, 405 U.S. 727 (1972); *Flast v. Cohen*, 392 U.S. 83 (1968).

12. Emile Durkheim, *The Division of Labor in Society* (New York: Free Press, 1933), 68.

13. This is a reference to "footnote 4" in Justice Stone's opinion in *United States v. Carolene Products Corporation*, 304 U.S. 144 (1938). See also John Hart Ely, *Democracy and Distrust* (Cambridge: Harvard University Press, 1980),

73–104, and Robert M. Cover, "The Origins of Judicial Activism in the Protection of Minorities," *Yale Law Journal* 91 (1982):1287.

14. *Personnel Administration v. Feeney*, 442 U.S. 256 (1979); *Craig v. Boren*, 429 U.S. 190 (1976); *San Antonio School District v. Rodriguez*, 411 U.S. 1 (1973); *Shapiro v. Thompson*, 394 U.S. 618 (1969).

15. Murray Edelman, *Political Language: Words That Succeed and Policies That Fail* (New York: Academic Press, 1977), 9, 74.

16. Vining, *Legal Identity*, 170–78.

17. Ibid., 59.

18. John Noonan, *Persons and Masks of the Law: Cardozo, Holmes, Jefferson, and Wythe as Makers of the Masks* (New York: Farrar, Straus & Giroux, 1976), 20.

19. Erich Fromm, *The Sane Society* (New York: Fawcett, 1955), 111.

20. Erich Fromm, *Marx's Concept of Man* (New York: Ungar, 1961), 44.

21. Ibid., 45.

22. Frantz Fanon, *Black Skin, White Masks* (New York: Grove Press, 1967), 8.

23. Erving Goffman, *The Presentation of Self in Everyday Life* (New York: Doubleday, 1959), 17–76.

24. George Santayana, *Soliloquies in England and Later Soliloquies* (New York: Scribner, 1922), 131–32.

25. Alan Freeman, "Legitimizing Racial Discrimination through Antidiscrimination Law: A Critical Review of Supreme Court Doctrine," *Minnesota Law Review* 62 (1978):1053.

26. Ibid., 1052–54.

27. See examples in Chapter 1.

28. Edelman, *Political Language*, 33, 35.

29. 163 U.S. 537 (1896).

30. Alan Freeman, "Anti-Discrimination Law: A Critical Review," in *The Politics of Law: A Progressive Critique*, ed. David Kairys (New York: Pantheon Books, 1982), 101.

31. Ralph Ellison, *Invisible Man* (New York: Vintage Books, 1947), 3.

32. *Franks v. Bowman Transportation Co.*, 424 U.S. 747 (1976), at 763, as interpreted in *Board of Regents of the University of California v. Bakke*, 438 U.S. 265 (1978), at 301. Emphasis added.

33. Kirchheimer, *Political Justice*, 110; he explains that trials "seal off the judgment of the past" and then reconstruct the incident, "torn from its history," with the simplicity and concreteness not found in past or future. The isolation of the incident by the trial assures that "[t]he past is reconstructed for the sake of the future as a possible weapon in the battle for political domination."

34. Fanon, *Black Skin, White Masks*, 230. Emphasis added.

35. *Board of Regents of the University of California v. Bakke*, 438 U.S. 265 (1978).

36. Ibid. at 294.

37. Ibid. at 295.

38. *Brown v. Board of Education of Topeka*, 347 U.S. 483 (1954), at 494.

39. Hannah Arendt, "Reflections on Little Rock," *Dissent* 6 (Winter 1959):45–46.

40. This conclusion is affirmed in Leon H. Mayhew, *Law and Equal Opportunity: A Study of the Massachusetts Commission against Discrimination* (Cambridge: Harvard University Press, 1968).

41. Alexander Bickel states the conventional view when he argues that the Court should follow the loosely defined goals of assimilation: see *The Least Dangerous Branch*, 2d ed. (New Haven: Yale University Press, 1968).

42. Michel Foucault, *Discipline and Punish: The Birth of the Prison* (New York: Vintage Books, 1979), 191–92. Emphasis added.

43. Specifically in the American context, Kai Erikson, *Wayward Puritans: A Study in the Sociology of Deviance* (New York: Wiley, 1966), 198, speaking of the Puritan "mask of disreputability," suggests: "Perhaps it is from the Puritans that we borrowed the odd rhetorical habit of saying about someone, 'he is an addict,' or 'he is a schizophrenic,' almost as if we were talking about his occupation. In many ways, this is precisely what the Puritans did mean by such a phrase: to characterize a person as deviant was to describe his spiritual condition, his calling, his vocation, his state of grace."

44. Ibid., 193.

45. Robert Coles, *Children of Crisis: A Study of Courage and Fear* (Boston: Little, Brown, 1964), 334.

46. Barrington Moore, Jr., *Injustice: The Social Bases of Obedience and Revolt* (New York: Sharpe, 1978), 13.

47. Georg Simmel, *Conflict and the Web of Group Affiliations* (New York: Free Press, 1955), 27.

48. Richard Flathman, *The Practice of Political Authority: Authority and the Authoritative* (Chicago: University of Chicago Press, 1980).

49. Frantz Fanon, *The Wretched of the Earth* (New York: Grove Press, 1963), 54.

50. Other attempts have been made to classify the psychological types of victims. The two most notable are Gordon Allport's "traits due to victimization": (1) ego defenses, (2) obsessive concern, (3) denial of membership, (4) withdrawal and passivity, (5) clowning, (6) strengthening in-group ties, (7) slyness and cunning, (8) self-hate, (9) aggression against one's own group, (10) prejudice against outside groups, (11) sympathy (for the prejudiced), (12) militancy, (13) symbolic status striving, and (14) neuroticism (*The Nature of Prejudice* [Boston: Beacon Press, 1954], 142–64), and Hans von Hentig's "psychological types of victims": (1) the depressed, (2) the acquisitive, (3) the wanton, (4) the lonesome and heartbroken, (5) the tormentor, and (6) blocked, exempted, and fighting victims (*The Criminal and His Victim* [1948; reprint, New York: Schocken Books, 1979], 419–37). These categories may be more effective at reinforcing stereotypes than providing a framework for analysis.

51. Simmel, *Conflict and the Web*, 39.

52. Herbert Marcuse, *Eros and Civilization* (New York: Vintage Books, 1955), 83.

53. Fanon, *Wretched of the Earth*, 53.

54. Eugene Genovese, *Roll, Jordan, Roll* (New York: Vintage Books, 1976), 6.

55. Ibid., 7.

56. Von Hentig, *Criminal and His Victim*, 419. Emphasis added.

57. Genovese, *Roll, Jordan, Roll*, 148–49.

58. Erikson, *Wayward Puritans*, 137–59.

59. Bruno Bettelheim, *Surviving and Other Essays* (New York: Vintage Books, 1980), 64, 67.

60. Genovese, *Roll, Jordan, Roll*, 74.

61. Susan Griffin, *Woman and Nature: The Roaring Inside Her* (New York: Harper & Row, 1978), 117–18. (The construction of sentences follows Griffin's literary style.)

62. Bettelheim, *Surviving*, 62.

63. Genovese, *Roll, Jordan, Roll*, 239.

64. Elizabeth Janeway, *Powers of the Weak* (New York: Morrow Quill, 1980), 117.

65. Ibid., 72.

66. Richard Sennett, *Authority* (New York: Vintage Books, 1980), 62–77.

67. Bettelheim, *Surviving*, 19–36.

68. Hannah Arendt, *Eichmann in Jerusalem: A Report on the Banality of Evil* (New York: Penguin Books, 1964), 37–55.

Five / The Ethic of Survival

1. These are three examples of structural constraints mentioned by the interviewees. For example, when an incident of discrimination ended with the individual's quitting or being fired from the job, the individual first dealt with unemployment compensation regulations.

2. How these constraints are transformed into "subjective" barriers is discussed in Chapter 6.

3. Beyond the specific examples that follow, it should be noted that institutional arrangements disadvantage minorities and women because they reinforce dominant interests. J. J. Gumperz nicely summarizes: "Minority group members do significantly less well than others in most spheres of institutional contact: in classroom interactions . . . , in large health care establishments, in relations with police and the courts, in counseling situations, and particularly in employment interviews. Although the interactive conditions involved in these situations vary in detail, they are similar in that what are ultimately judged are such matters as coherence of arguments, validity of justification, and persuasiveness of requests." "The Communicative Bases of Social Inequality," in *Minorities: Communities and Identity*, ed. C. Fried (Berlin: Springer-Verlag, 1983), 117.

4. For this interpretation of authority, see Barrington Moore, Jr., *Injustice: The Social Bases of Obedience and Revolt* (New York: Sharpe, 1978), 15–30. For a contrasting interpretation of the morality of authority, see John Rawls, *A Theory of Justice* (Cambridge: Harvard University Press, 1971), 462–67.

5. Psychological studies have found a disconcertingly high level of submission to authority; for example, Stanley Milgram, *Obedience to Authority: An Experimental View* (New York: Harper & Row, 1974). Studies also link American cultural values and support for authority: see Fred Greenstein, *Children and Politics* (New Haven: Yale University Press, 1969); Gabriel Almond and Sidney Verba, *The Civic Culture Revisited* (Boston: Little, Brown, 1980). For a discussion of the problem of legitimacy and authority, see Theodore Lowi, *The End of Liberalism: The Second Republic of the United States* (New York: Norton, 1979), and Alan Wolfe, *The Limits of Legitimacy: Political Contradictions of Contemporary Capitalism* (New York: Free Press, 1978).

6. Niccolò Machiavelli, *The Prince*, in *Masterworks of Government*, ed. L. D. Abbott (New York: McGraw-Hill, 1947), 157: "Therefore a prince, so long as he keeps his subjects united and loyal, ought not to mind the reproach of cruelty." The answer to whether it is not better to be feared than loved is that "fear preserves you by a dread of punishment that never fails."

7. Ibid., 162. In the context of the entire quotation, the prince need not have virtuous qualities; he must only *appear* to have them: "Let a prince have the credit of conquering and holding his state, the means will be praised by everybody, because the vulgar are always taken by what a thing seems to be and by what comes of it; and in the world there are only the vulgar, for the few find a place there only when the many have no ground to rest on."

8. Gordon W. Allport, *The Nature of Prejudice* (Boston: Beacon Press, 1954), 506.

9. Allport cites two studies showing that proprietors of restaurants and hotels are more likely to report that they would discriminate than they are, in fact, to engage in acts of discrimination. The conclusions were that discrimination is less likely to occur if there is a face-to-face confrontation. See Allport, p. 56, and his citations.

10. I am not implying that these were real acts of "choice," given the potential for retaliation, only that the sequence of events is predetermined when the persons who suffer from hostile treatment back off from the potential confrontation.

11. Hannah Arendt, *Rahel Varnhagen: The Life of a Jewish Woman* (New York: Harcourt Brace Jovanovich, 1974), 3.

12. Ibid., 4.
13. Ibid., 6.
14. Ibid., 7.
15. Ibid., 8.
16. Ibid., 8.
17. Ibid., 9.
18. Ibid., 11.

19. For a discussion of Rahel's flight from identity as revealed in her letter writing, see Liliane Weissberg, "Writing on the Wall: Letters of Rahel Varnhagen," *New German Critique* 36 (1985):157–73.

20. Arendt, *Rahel Varnhagen*, 120.
21. Ibid., 220.

22. Malcolm X, *The Autobiography of Malcolm X* (New York: Ballantine Books, 1965), 1–22.

23. Ibid., 34–38.

24. Ibid., 84–107.

25. Ibid., 236–65.

26. Eugene Victor Wolfenstein, *The Victims of Democracy: Malcolm X and the Black Revolution* (Berkeley and Los Angeles: University of California Press, 1981), 19.

27. Sylvia lives in a one-room apartment in an overcrowded section of downtown Los Angeles (the conditions are particularly bad because many of the tenants are illegals).

28. For a discussion of how people endure stress and discrimination, see Robert Coles, *Children of Crisis: A Study of Courage and Fear* (Boston: Little, Brown, 1964), 346.

29. Georg Lukács, speaking of the bureaucrat's conscientiousness, sees that it is "precisely his 'honor' and his 'sense of responsibility' that exact his total submission. . . . It points to the fact that the division of labor. . . invades the realm of ethics. . . . This strengthens the reified structure of consciousness. . . as long as the fate of the worker still appears to be an individual fate." *History and Class Consciousness: Studies in Marxist Dialectics* (Cambridge: MIT Press, 1968), 99–100.

30. Carmen draws a connection between pride and powerlessness: "I thought I was treated unfairly. I knew I was being cheated out of something I should have had. At a very young age, somewhere along the line I got this thing, that I will tell my children. In order to like anybody else, you have to like yourself. When I am special to me, I am special to other people."

31. I am suggesting that, in general, the moral content of antidiscrimination law is ambiguous. The growing tendency of law to lose its ethical content is addressed as a formal quality of modern law in Max Weber, *Economy and Society*, ed. Guenther Roth and Claus Wittich (Berkeley and Los Angeles: University of California Press, 1968), 2:884–85.

32. Judith Farr Tormey, in a philosophical analysis of the concepts of exploitation and oppression, concludes: "We can see how self-sacrificing behavior complements exploitation. The exploiter acts with too little respect for the interests of others; conversely the self-sacrificer acts with too little respect for his/her interests, thus offering little resistance to exploitation." The means of exploitation is the adoption of the "morality of self-sacrifice," which convinces people that they must consistently give more weight to the interests of others than to their own. See "Exploitation, Oppression, and Self-Sacrifice," in *Women and Philosophy: Toward a Theory of Liberation*, ed. Carol C. Gould and Marx W. Wartofsky (New York: Putnam, 1976), 221, 219.

33. This problem has been described by Jean Elshtain as the women's difficulty in transcending the public-private distinction. Elshtain argues that women face a perpetual double bind: they have "natural" concerns arising from the private sphere, but if they join the dialogue of power politics to further those interests they have forsaken their private values. This analysis refers

specifically to the suffragists' difficulties in transcending the public-private distinction in their struggle for "formal-legalistic equality." Elshtain's account reveals how women acting in public roles are similar to my respondents in their inability to transcend the private dimension of their lives. See "Moral Woman and Immoral Man: A Consideration of the Public-Private Split and Its Political Ramifications," *Politics and Society* 4 (1974): 453–73.

34. Richard Sennett, *Authority* (New York: Vintage Books, 1980), 196.

35. There is also a more generalizable sociological theory of rights, "the chance of support by the apparatus of force of the state for the power of command." Weber, *Economy and Society*, 666–67.

36. This discussion of Weber's sociology of rights and its relationship to struggles for survival is drawn from the analysis in Ralf Dahrendorf, *Life Chances: Approaches to Social and Political Theory* (Chicago: University of Chicago Press, 1979), 62–74.

37. Ibid., 71.

38. *Runjon v. McCrary*, 427 U.S. 160 (1976).

39. *Smith v. Allwright*, 321 U.S. 649 (1944).

40. *Board of Regents of the University of California v. Bakke*, 438 U.S. 649 (1978).

41. Delma also makes reference to her impression that she can use the expression "There are laws against that sort of thing" only as a joke (Chapter 6).

42. This model of conflict is found in Ralf Dahrendorf, *Class and Class Conflict in Industrial Society* (Stanford: Stanford University Press, 1959). Yet, this model is consistent with pluralistic notions of political reform.

43. Murray Edelman, *Political Language: Words That Succeed and Policies That Fail* (New York: Academic Press, 1977), 133–36.

44. See Frances F. Piven and Richard A. Cloward, *Regulating the Poor: The Functions of Public Welfare* (New York: Vintage Books, 1971); Albert O. Hirschman, *Shifting Involvements: Private Interest and Public Action* (Princeton: Princeton University Press, 1982); Anthony Downs, "Up and Down with Ecology—The Issue Attention Cycle," *Public Interest* 28 (1972):38–50.

45. Hannah Arendt, *The Human Condition* (Chicago: University of Chicago Press, 1958), 243.

Six / Legality Enters Life

1. The model of legal protection assumes a "double institutionalization" of legal norms (Paul Bohannon, "Law," in *International Encyclopedia of the Social Sciences* (New York: Macmillan, 1968), 73–78. The phrase describes the process by which legal norms are anticipated or incorporated into social rules. Bohannon suggests that law reinforces custom and common morality. In the case of discrimination, this suggests that legal sanctions inhibit discriminatory behavior when those in a position to discriminate acknowledge the power of the law. One critic of Bohannon suggests that law and custom do not constitute a continuous process that promotes legal change, but instead that there is a complex interaction between law, society, and the state (Stanley Diamond, "The Rule of

Law versus the Order of Custom," in *The Rule of Law*, ed. Robert Paul Wolff (New York: Simon & Schuster, 1971), 115–46.

2. See, for example, Boaventura de Sousa Santos, "The Law of the Oppressed: The Construction and Reproduction of Legality in Pasargada," *Law and Society Review* 12 (1977):7.

3. See, for a different statement about the paradoxes created by law, Daniel J. Boorstin, "The Perils of Indwelling Law," in *The Rule of Law*, ed. Robert Paul Wolff (New York: Simon & Schuster, 1971), 75–97.

4. Hanna Pitkin, *Wittgenstein and Justice: On the Significance of Ludwig Wittgenstein for Social and Political Thought* (Berkeley and Los Angeles: University of California Press, 1972), 169–92.

5. Alexis de Tocqueville, *Democracy in America*, ed. Francis Bowen (New York: Knopf, 1956), 1:264.

6. Niklas Luhmann, in his analysis of communications about law in "interaction systems," developed a model that can be adapted for interpreting the reluctant use of legal themes by victims of discrimination. Luhmann is interested in legal issues that arise in *conflicts*, a particular type of social situation. Once an interaction becomes a conflict, legal themes may potentially monopolize and focus communication. If the conflict is legalized, it both institutionalizes a binary structure, in which all aspects of the conflict are seen in terms of right and wrong, and forces a "role-taking" position, in which the disputant defends the introduction of law. This model of the communication process explains why participants would choose, once they encounter conflict, to "de-thematize" the interaction (Niklas Luhmann, "Communication about Law in Interactional Systems," in *Advances in Social Theory and Methodology: Toward an Integration of Micro- and Macro-Sociology*, ed. K. Knorr-Cetina and A. V. Cicourel [Boston: Routledge & Kegan Paul, 1981], 234–56).

The introduction of the legal theme transforms the conflict so that the participants, in order to prevail in a dispute, require support for outside authorities. In Luhmann's model, all legal culture is based on "the separation at the primary interactional level of questions of power from those of law, and the reformulation of their relationship on the macro-level of the total society. Decisions about legal issues become the province of a distant authority, one that has no direct connection with the interactionally present, immediately available power of the participating actors" (244). In some cases, law can be advantageous to the weaker parties because it removes law to a rule-oriented context that favors the disadvantaged. But, as Luhmann continues, "it also makes thematization more difficult: when someone turns something into a legal issue, he thereby indicates that he is not dependent on the motive structure of the concrete interaction of which he is part.... *Not all interaction systems can handle this kind of alienation*" (244–45, emphasis added). Legal thematization rudely displaces the power relations in the social situation (for better or worse).

7. What are the consequences for the parties involved once the foreign intervention of the law has occurred? The conflict that is brought into the sphere of the legal system may be structured by forms of communication that are incompatible with the way parties interact in everyday life. In particular,

the rigidity of legal themes can be offensive to usual means of communication. As a consequence, people will avoid the "thematization of law," resulting in the "drying up of the legal system" and the resolution of conflict by "other mechanisms—e.g., morality, ignorance, class structure, or the use of force outside the law—whose social structural compatibility may be problematic" (ibid., 247). Luhmann's model of communication interaction systems explains how the incompatibility of legal themes with communication in everyday life may reinforce power structures outside of the law.

8. Franz Kafka, *The Trial* (New York: Schocken Books, 1968), 222.

9. Ibid., 213.

10. Ibid., 215.

11. Erich Heller, *The Disinherited Mind: Essays in Modern German Literature and Thought* (New York: Harcourt Brace Jovanovich, 1975), 199–200.

12. The person's relationship with the law creates a false sense of autonomy. As one commentator writes in reference to Kafka's short story "The Hunger Artist," the victim "becomes enslaved by his 'thirst' for autonomy at the moment of choice. He is a consensual slave to his moment-to-moment passion for self-control, and he eventually allows that passion to destroy him." Robin West, "Authority, Autonomy, and Choice: The Role of Consent in the Moral and Political Visions of Franz Kafka and Richard Posner," *Harvard Law Review* 99 (1985):394.

13. Kafka, *The Trial*, 20.

Seven / Conclusion: Voices Excluded from the Law

1. Offe offers a hypothetical example of the effects of legal intervention in a situation in which the Fourteenth Amendment is applied to a dispute between a husband and wife. He hypothesizes that "if the conflict is transferred into the realm of legal regulation, and if one of the partners says, 'According to the Fourteenth Amendment to the Family Act, husband and wife are equally entitled to. . .', the conflict is not resolved. . . .The very recourse to legal regulations violates principles of mutual recognition, encourages cynicism between actors, and may even encourage them to retaliate by 'escaping' the consequences of the law. . . .By encouraging calculative modes of problem-solving, which do not necessarily produce the desired outcomes, this type of formal-legal regulation is self-undermining." *Contradictions of the Welfare State* (Cambridge: MIT Press, 1984), 281. Despite the fact that Offe does not address the reinforcement of inequalities, his hypothetical example is supported by my observations of victims of discrimination.

2. Malcolm Feeley, "The Effects of Heavy Caseloads," in *American Court Systems*, ed. Sheldon Goldman and Austin Sarat (San Francisco: Freeman, 1978), 118. See also *The Process Is the Punishment* (New York: Russell Sage Foundation, 1979).

3. See, for example, the use of the phrase in Gerda Lerner, *Black Women in White America* (New York: Vintage Books, 1972), 287.

4. The paradox of irrationality is a concept employed in William K. Muir's study of police behavior, *Police: Streetcorner Politicians* (Chicago: University of Chicago Press, 1977). To express the political uses of irrationality he quotes Alexis de Tocqueville's *Recollections*: "I have always thought that in revolutions, especially democratic revolutions, madmen (not those metaphorically called such, but real madmen) have played a very considerable political part. At least it is certain that at such times a state of semi-madness is not out of place and often leads to success" (126).

5. Robert Pear, "Civil Rights Act Is Assessed as 'Modest' Step," *New York Times*, 1 July 1984.

6. Derrick Bell, "Foreword: The Civil Rights Chronicles," *Harvard Law Review* 98 (November 1985):1–85.

7. Owen Fiss, "Groups and the Equal Protection Clause," in *Equality and Preferential Treatment*, ed. Marshall Cohen, Thomas Nagel, and Thomas Scanlon (Princeton: Princeton University Press, 1977), 85–154.

8. Ibid., 123.

9. Ibid., 97.

Bibliography

Allport, Gordon W. *The Nature of Prejudice*. Boston: Beacon Press, 1954.

Almond, Gabriel, and Sidney Verba. *The Civic Culture Revisited*. Boston: Little, Brown, 1980.

Almquist, Elisabeth M. "Women in the Labor Force." *Signs* 2 (1977):843–55.

Andreasen, Alan. *The Disadvantaged Consumer*. New York: Free Press, 1975.

Arendt, Hannah. *The Human Condition*. Chicago: University of Chicago Press, 1958.

———. "Reflections on Little Rock." *Dissent* 6 (Winter 1959):45–56.

———. *Eichmann in Jerusalem: A Report on the Banality of Evil*. New York: Penguin Books, 1964.

———. *Rahel Varnhagen: The Life of a Jewish Woman*. New York: Harcourt Brace Jovanovich, 1974.

Arrow, Kenneth. "Models of Job Discrimination." In *Racial Discrimination in Economic Life*, edited by Anthony H. Pascal. Lexington, Mass.: Lexington Books, 1972.

Balbus, Isaac D. *The Dialectics of Legal Repression: Black Rebels before the American Criminal Courts*. New York: Russell Sage Foundation, 1973.

Beauvoir, Simone de. *The Ethics of Ambiguity*. Secaucus, N.J.: Citadel Press, 1980.

Becker, Gary S. *The Economics of Discrimination*. Chicago: University of Chicago Press, 1957.

Bell, Derrick. "Foreword: The Civil Rights Chronicles." *Harvard Law Review* 98 (December 1985):4–83.

Bennett, W. Lance. "The Paradox of Public Discourse: A Framework for the Analysis of Political Accounts." *Journal of Politics* 42 (1979):792–817.

Bennett, W. Lance, and Martha S. Feldman. *Restructuring Reality in the Courtroom*. New Brunswick: Rutgers University Press, 1981.

Berger, Morroe. *Equality by Statute*. New York: Doubleday, 1967.

Berger, Raoul. *Government by Judiciary: The Transformation of the Fourteenth Amendment*. Cambridge: Harvard University Press, 1977.

Bestor, Arthur. "The American Civil War as a Constitutional Crisis." *American Historical Review* 69 (1964):327–52.

Bettelheim, Bruno. *Surviving and Other Essays*. New York: Vintage Books, 1980.

Bickel, Alexander. *The Least Dangerous Branch*. 2d ed. New Haven: Yale University Press, 1968.

Black, Donald. "The Mobilization of Law." *Journal of Legal Studies* 2 (1973):125–49.

———. *The Behavior of Law*. New York: Academic Press, 1976.

Blumberg, Abraham. "The Practice of Law as a Confidence Game: The Organizational Cooptation of a Profession." *Law and Society Review* 1 (1967):15–39.

Blumrosen, Ruth G. "Wage Discrimination, Job Segregation, and Title VII of the Civil Rights Act of 1964." *University of Michigan Journal of Law Reform* 12 (1979):397–502.

Boggs, James. *Racism and the Class Struggle: Further Pages from a Black Worker's Notebook*. New York: Monthly Review Press, 1970.

Bohannon, Paul. "Law." In *International Encyclopedia of the Social Sciences*, 73–78. New York: Macmillan, 1968.

Boorstin, Daniel J. *The Decline of Radicalism: Reflections on America Today*. New York: Random House, 1969.

———. "The Perils of Indwelling Law." In *The Rule of Law*, edited by Robert Paul Wolff, 75–97. New York: Simon & Schuster, 1971.

Brophy, Julia, and Carol Smart, eds. *Women in Law*. London: Routledge & Kegan Paul, 1985.

Bumiller, Kristin. "Victims in the Shadow of the Law: A Critique of the Model of Legal Protection." *Signs* 12 (Spring 1987):421–53.

Burns, W. Hayward. "Race Discrimination Law and Race in America." In *The Politics of Law: A Progressive Critique*, edited by David Kairys, 89–95. New York: Pantheon Books, 1982.

Burstein, Paul, and Kathleen Monaghan. "Equal Employment Opportunity and the Mobilization of Law." *Law and Society Review* 20 (1986):355–88.

Carmichael, Stokely, and Charles V. Hamilton. *Black Power: The Politics of Liberation in America*. New York: Vintage Books, 1967.

Carson, Claybourne. *In Struggle: SNCC and the Black Awakening of the 1960s*. Cambridge: Harvard University Press, 1981.

Chayes, Abram. "The Role of the Judge in Public Law Litigation." *Harvard Law Review* 89 (1976):1281–1316.

Coates, Dan, and Steven Penrod. "Social Psychology and the Emergence of Disputes." *Law and Society Review* 15 (1980–81):655–80.

Cohen, William. "Negro Involuntary Servitude in the South, 1865–1940." *Journal of Southern History* 42 (1976):31–60.

Coles, Robert. *Children of Crisis: A Study of Courage and Fear*. Boston: Little, Brown, 1964.

Collier, Jane. *Law and Social Change in Zinacantan*. Stanford: Stanford University Press, 1973.

Cover, Robert M. *Justice Accused: Anti-Slavery and the Judicial Process*. New Haven: Yale University Press, 1975.

———. "The Origins of Judicial Activism in the Protection of Minorities." *Yale Law Journal* 91 (1982):1287–1316.

Crenshaw, Kimberle. "Race, Reform, and Retrenchment: Transformation and Legitimation in Antidiscrimination Law." *Harvard Law Review* 101, forthcoming, December 1987.

Crosskey, William Winslow. *Politics and the Constitution in the History of the United States*. Chicago: University of Chicago Press, 1951.

Crowe, Patricia Ward. "Complainant Reactions to the Massachusetts Commission against Discrimination." *Law and Society Review* 12 (1978):217–35.

Currie, Elliott. "Crimes without Criminals: Witchcraft and Its Control in Renaissance Europe." *Law and Society Review* 3 (1968):7–32.

Dahrendorf, Ralf. *Class and Class Conflict in Industrial Society*. Stanford: Stanford University Press, 1959.

———. *Life Chances: Approaches to Social and Political Theory*. Chicago: University of Chicago Press, 1979.

Daniel, Pete. "The Metamorphosis of Slavery, 1865–1900." *Journal of American History* 66 (1978):88–89.

Diamond, Stanley. "The Rule of Law versus the Order of Custom." In *The Rule of Law*, edited by Robert Paul Wolff, 115–44. New York: Simon & Schuster, 1971.

Downs, Anthony. "Up and Down with Ecology—The Issue Attention Cycle." *Public Interest* 28 (1972):38–50.

Durkheim, Emile. *The Division of Labor in Society*. New York: Free Press, 1933.

Edelman, Murray. *Political Language: Words That Succeed and Policies That Fail*. New York: Academic Press, 1977.

———. "Art as Liberating Political Communication." *Institut für Höhere Studien* 6 (1982):1–15.

Engel, David, and Eric Steele. "Civil Cases and Society: Process and Order in the Civil Justice System." *American Bar Foundation Research Journal* 1979 (Spring):295–346.

Elkins, Stanley M. *Slavery: A Problem in American Institutional and Intellectual Life*. Chicago: University of Chicago Press, 1959.

Ellison, Ralph. *Invisible Man*. New York: Vintage Books, 1947.

Elshtain, Jean B. "Moral Woman and Immoral Man: A Consideration of the Public-Private Split and Its Political Ramifications." *Politics and Society* 4 (1974):453–73.

Ely, John Hart. *Democracy and Distrust: A Theory of Judicial Review*. Cambridge: Harvard University Press, 1980.

Erikson, Kai. *Wayward Puritans: A Study in the Sociology of Deviance*. New York: Wiley, 1966.

Fager, Charles. *Selma 1965: The March That Changed the South*. Boston: Beacon Press, 1985.

Fanon, Frantz. *The Wretched of the Earth*. New York: Grove Press, 1963.

———. *Black Skin, White Masks*. New York: Grove Press, 1967.

Feeley, Malcolm. "The Effects of Heavy Caseloads." In *American Court Systems*, edited by Sheldon Goldman and Austin Sarat, 110–18. San Francisco: Freeman, 1978.

———. *The Process Is the Punishment*. New York: Russell Sage Foundation, 1979.

Felstiner, William. "The Influences of Social Organization on Dispute Processing." *Law and Society Review* 9 (1974):63–94.

Ferber, Marianne A., and Helen M. Lowry. "Women: The New Reserve Army of the Unemployed." *Signs* 1 (1976):213–32.

Fineman, Martha L. "Implementing Equality: Ideology, Contradiction, and Social Change. A Study of Rhetoric and Result in the Regulation of the Consequences of Divorce." *Wisconsin Law Review*, 1983, no. 4:789–886.

Fiss, Owen. "Groups and the Equal Protection Clause." In *Equality and Preferential Treatment*, edited by Marshall Cohen, Thomas Nagel, and

Thomas Scanlon, 84–154. Princeton: Princeton University Press, 1977.

———. "School Desegregation: The Uncertain Path of the Law." In *Equality and Preferential Treatment*, edited by Marshall Cohen, Thomas Nagel, and Thomas Scanlon, 155–91. Princeton: Princeton University Press, 1977.

———. "Foreword: The Forms of Justice." *Harvard Law Review* 93 (1979):1–58.

Flathman, Richard. *The Practice of Political Authority: Authority and the Authoritative*. Chicago: University of Chicago Press, 1980.

Foucault, Michel. *Discipline and Punish: The Birth of the Prison*. New York: Vintage Books, 1979.

———. *Power/Knowledge*. New York: Pantheon Books, 1980.

Frank, Jerome. *Law and the Modern Mind*. New York: Brentano's, 1930.

Franklin, John Hope. *Reconstruction after the Civil War*. Chicago: University of Chicago Press, 1961.

Freeman, Alan. "Legitimizing Discrimination through Anti-Discrimination Law: A Critical Review of Supreme Court Doctrine." *Minnesota Law Review* 62 (1978):1049–1119.

———. "Anti-Discrimination Law: A Critical Review." In *The Politics of Law: A Progressive Critique*, edited by David Kairys, 96–116. New York: Pantheon Books, 1982.

Fromm, Erich. *The Sane Society*. New York: Fawcett, 1955.

———. *Marx's Concept of Man*. New York: Ungar, 1961.

Fuller, Lon. "The Forms and Limits of Adjudication." *Harvard Law Review* 92 (1978):353–409.

———. "American Legal Realism." *University of Pennsylvania Law Review* 82 (1934):429–62.

Geertz, Clifford. *The Interpretation of Cultures*. New York: Basic Books, 1973.

———. "Blurred Genres: The Reconfiguration of Social Thought." Chap. 1 in *Local Knowledge: Further Essays in Interpretive Anthropology*. New York: Basic Books, 1983.

Genovese, Eugene. *Roll, Jordan, Roll*. New York: Vintage Books, 1976.

Gilligan, Carol. *In a Different Voice: Psychological Theory and Women's Development*. Cambridge: Harvard University Press, 1982.

Glazer, Nathan. *Affirmative Discrimination: Ethnic Inequality and Public Policy*. New York: Basic Books, 1975.

Goffman, Erving. *The Presentation of Self in Everyday Life*. New York: Doubleday, 1959.

———. *Stigma: Notes on the Management of Spoiled Identity*. Englewood Cliffs, N.J.: Prentice-Hall, 1963.

Goldman, Alan H. *Justice and Reverse Discrimination*. Princeton: Princeton University Press, 1979.

Greenstein, Fred. *Children and Politics*. New Haven: Yale University Press, 1969.

Griffin, Susan. *Woman and Nature: The Roaring Inside Her*. New York: Harper & Row, 1978.

Gulliver, Philip H. *Disputes and Negotiations: A Cross-Cultural Perspective*. New York: Academic Press, 1979.

Gumperz, J. J. "The Communicative Bases of Social Inequality." In *Minorities: Communities and Identity*, edited by C. Fried. Berlin: Springer-Verlag, 1983.

Gurin, Patricia. "The Role of Worker Expectancies in the Study of Employment Discrimination." In *Women, Minorities, and Employment Discrimination*, edited by Phyllis A. Wallace and Annette M. LaMond. Lexington, Mass.: Lexington Books, 1977.

Hagen, John, and Kristin Bumiller. "Making Sense of Sentencing." In *Research on Sentencing: The Search for Reform*, edited by Alfred Blumstein, 2:1–54. Washington, D.C.: National Academy Press, 1983.

Handler, Joel. *Social Movements and the Legal System*. New York: Academic Press, 1978.

Hay, Douglas, et al., eds. *Albion's Fatal Tree: Crime and Society in Eighteenth-Century England*. New York: Pantheon Books, 1975.

Heller, Erich. *Franz Kafka*. Princeton: Princeton University Press, 1974.

———. *The Disinherited Mind: Essays in Modern German Literature and Thought*. New York: Harcourt Brace Jovanovich, 1975.

Hentig, Hans von. *The Criminal and His Victim: Studies in the Sociobiology of Crime*. 1948. Reprint. New York: Schocken Books, 1979.

Hirschman, Albert O. *Exit, Voice, and Loyalty: Responses to Decline in Firms, Organizations, and States*. Cambridge: Harvard University Press, 1970.

———. *Shifting Involvements: Private Interest and Public Action*. Princeton: Princeton University Press, 1982.

Hochschild, Jennifer. *What's Fair? American Beliefs about Distributive Justice*. Cambridge: Harvard University Press, 1981.

Horowitz, Donald. *The Courts and Social Policy*. Washington, D.C.: Brookings Institution, 1977.

Horwitz, Morton. *The Transformation of American Law, 1780–1860*. Cambridge: Harvard University Press, 1977.

Hunt, Alan. "The Ideology of Law: Advances and Problems in Recent Applications of the Concept of Ideology to the Analysis of Law." *Law and Society Review* 19 (1985):1–37.

Hyman, Harold, and William M. Wiecek. *Equal Justice under Law: Constitutional Development, 1835–1875*. New York: Harper & Row, 1982.

Janeway, Elizabeth. *Powers of the Weak*. New York: Morrow, 1980.

Kafka, Franz. *The Trial*. New York: Schocken Books, 1968.

Kairys, David, ed. *The Politics of Law: A Progressive Critique*. New York: Pantheon Books, 1982.

Kennedy, Duncan. "Toward an Historical Understanding of Legal Consciousness: The Case of Classical Legal Thought in America, 1850–1940." *Research in Law and Sociology* 3 (1980):3–24.

King, Martin Luther, Jr. *Stride toward Freedom*, 1958. Excerpted in *The Civil Rights Reader*, edited by Leon Friedman. New York: Walker, 1968.

Kirchheimer, Otto. *Political Justice: The Use of Legal Procedure for Political Ends*. Princeton: Princeton University Press, 1961.

Kritzer, Herbert. "Studying Disputes: Learning from the CLRP Experience." *Law and Society Review* 15 (1980–81):503–24.

Kutler, Stanley. *Judicial Power and Reconstruction Politics.* Chicago: University of Chicago Press, 1968.

Lane, Robert. *Political Ideology: Why the American Common Man Believes What He Does.* New York: Free Press, 1962.

Lemert, Charles C., and Garth C. Gillan. *Michel Foucault: Social Theory as Transgression.* New York: Columbia University Press, 1982.

Lerner, Gerda. *Black Women in White America.* New York: Vintage Books, 1972.

Llewellyn, Karl, and E. Adamson Hoebel. *The Cheyenne Way: Conflict and Case Law in Primitive Jurisprudence.* Norman: University of Oklahoma Press, 1941.

Lofland, John. *Analyzing Social Settings: A Guide to Qualitative Observation and Analysis.* Belmont, Calif.: Wadsworth, 1971.

Loury, Glen C. "A Dynamic Theory of Racial Income Differences." In *Women, Minorities, and Employment Discrimination,* edited by Phyllis A. Wallace and Annette M. LaMond. Lexington, Mass.: Lexington Books, 1977.

Lowi, Theodore. *The End of Liberalism: The Second Republic of the United States.* New York: Norton, 1979.

Luhmann, Niklas. "Communication about Law in Interactional Systems." In *Advances in Social Theory and Methodology: Toward an Integration of Micro- and Macro-Sociology,* edited by K. Knorr-Cetina and A. V. Cicourel, 234–56. Boston: Routledge & Kegan Paul, 1981.

Lukács, Georg. *History and Class Consciousness: Studies in Marxist Dialectics.* Cambridge: MIT Press, 1968.

Macauley, Stewart. "Non-Contractual Relations in Business: A Preliminary Study." *American Sociological Review* 28 (1963):55–67.

McCrone, Donald J., and Richard J. Hardy. "Civil Rights and the Achievement of Racial Economic Equality, 1948–1975." *American Journal of Political Science* 22 (1978):1–17.

Machiavelli, Niccolò. *The Prince.* In *Masterworks in Government,* edited by L. D. Abbott. New York: McGraw-Hill, 1947.

MacKinnon, Catharine. *Sexual Harrassment of Working Women: A Case of Sex Discrimination.* New Haven: Yale University Press, 1979.

Malcolm X. *The Autobiography of Malcolm X.* New York: Ballantine Books, 1965.

Mannheim, Karl. *Ideology and Utopia: An Introduction to the Sociology of Knowledge.* New York: Harcourt, Brace, 1936.

Marcus, Isabel, et al. "Feminist Discourse, Moral Values, and the Law—A Conversation." *Buffalo Law Review* 34 (1985):11–87.

Marcuse, Herbert. *Eros and Civilization.* New York: Vintage Books, 1955.

———. *One-dimensional Man.* Boston: Beacon Press, 1964.

———. *The Aesthetic Dimension.* Boston: Beacon Press, 1977.

Mather, Lynn, and Barbara Yngvesson. "Language, Audience, and the Transformation of Disputes." *Law and Society Review* 15 (1980–81):773–821.

Mayhew, Leon. *Law and Equal Opportunity: A Study of the Massachusetts Commission against Discrimination.* Cambridge: Harvard University Press, 1968.

Merry, Sally. "Going to Court: Strategies of Dispute Management in an Urban American Neighborhood." *Law and Society Review* 13 (1979):891–924.

———. "Concepts of Law and Justice among Working Class Americans: Ideology as Culture." *Legal Studies Forum* 9 (1985):59–70.

Merry, Sally, and Susan S. Silbey. "What Do Plaintiffs Want? Re-examining the Concept of Dispute." *Justice System Journal* 9 (1984):151–178.

Milgram, Stanley. *Obedience to Authority: An Experimental View.* New York: Harper & Row, 1974.

Mnookin, Robert M., and Lewis Kornhauser. "Bargaining in the Shadow of the Law: The Case of Divorce." *Yale Law Journal* 88 (1979):950–97.

Moore, Barrington, Jr. *The Social Origins of Dictatorship and Democracy: Lord and Peasant in the Making of the Modern World.* Boston: Beacon Press, 1966.

———. *Injustice: The Social Basis of Obedience and Revolt.* New York: Sharpe, 1978.

Morris, Aldon D. *The Origins of the Civil Rights Movement: Black Communities Organizing for Change.* New York: Free Press, 1981.

Muir, William K. *Police: Streetcorner Politicians.* Chicago: University of Chicago Press, 1977.

Myrdal, Gunnar. *An American Dilemma: The Negro Problem and Modern Democracy.* New York: McGraw-Hill, 1944.

Nader, Laura, and Harry F. Todd, eds. *The Disputing Process: Law in Ten Societies.* New York: Columbia University Press, 1978.

Noonan, John. *Persons and Masks of the Law: Cardozo, Holmes, Jefferson, and Wyhe as Makers of the Masks.* New York: Farrar, Straus & Giroux, 1976.

Offe, Claus. "Structural Problems of the Capitalist State." *German Political Studies* 1 (1974):31–56.

———. *Contradictions of the Welfare State.* Cambridge: MIT Press, 1984.

Pear, Robert. "Civil Rights Act Is Assessed as 'Modest' Step." *New York Times,* 1 July 1984.

Pitkin, Hanna. *Wittgenstein and Justice: On the Significance of Ludwig Wittgenstein for Social and Political Thought.* Berkeley and Los Angeles: University of California Press, 1972.

Piven, Frances F., and Richard Cloward. *Regulating the Poor: The Functions of Public Welfare.* New York: Vintage Books, 1971.

Platt, Anthony. *The Child Savers: The Invention of Delinquency.* Chicago: University of Chicago Press, 1977.

Poulantzas, Nicos. *State, Power, and Socialism.* London: NLB, 1978.

Powers, Kathryn L. "Sex Segregation and the Ambivalent Directions of Sex Discrimination Law." *Wisconsin Law Review,* 1979, no. 1:55–124.

Psathas, George, ed. *Everyday Language: Studies in Ethnomethodology.* New York: Wiley, 1979.

Quinney, Richard. *Class, State, and Crime.* 2d ed. New York: Longman, 1980.

Rawls, John. *A Theory of Justice.* Cambridge: Harvard University Press, 1971.

Riegel, Stephen J. "The Persistent Career of Jim Crow: Lower Federal Courts and the Separate But Equal Doctrine, 1865–1896." *American Journal of Legal History* 28 (1984):17–40.

Rodgers, Harrel R., Jr., and Charles S. Bullock III. *Law and Social Change: Civil Rights Laws and Their Consequences.* New York: McGraw-Hill, 1972.

Rose, Willie Lee. *Slavery and Freedom.* New York: Oxford University Press, 1982.

Ross, H. Laurence. *Settled Out of Court: The Social Process of Insurance Claim Adjustment.* Chicago: Aldine, 1979.

Santayana, George. *Soliloquies in England and Later Soliloquies.* New York: Scribner, 1922.

Santos, Boaventura de Sousa. "The Law of the Oppressed: The Construction and Reproduction of Legality in Pasargada." *Law and Society Review* 12 (1977):5–126.

———. "Law and Community: The Changing Nature of State Power in Late Capitalism." *International Journal of the Sociology of Law* 8 (1980):379–97.

———. "Science and Politics: Doing Research in Rio's Squatter Settlements." In *Law and Social Enquiry,* edited by Robin Luchman, 261–81. Uppsala: Scandinavian Institute of African Studies, 1981.

———. "On Modes of Production of Social Power and Law." Institute for Legal Studies Working Paper, vol. 1, no. 1, Law School, University of Wisconsin-Madison, 1985.

Sawhill, Isabel. "Discrimination and Poverty among Women Who Head Families." *Signs* 1 (1976):201–11.

Scheingold, Stuart. *The Politics of Rights: Lawyers, Public Policy, and Political Change.* New Haven: Yale University Press, 1974.

Scott, Robert L., and Wayne Brockriede, eds. *The Rhetoric of Black Power.* New York: Harper & Row, 1969.

Scull, Andrew T. *Decarceration: Community Treatment and the Deviant—A Radical View.* Englewood Cliffs, N.J.: Prentice-Hall, 1977.

Sennett, Richard. *Authority.* New York: Vintage Books, 1980.

Simmel, Georg. *Conflict and the Web of Group Affiliations.* New York: Free Press, 1955.

Simon, William. "The Ideology of Advocacy: Procedural Justice and Professional Ethics." *Wisconsin Law Review,* 1978, no. 1:29–144.

Smith, Arthur B., Charles B. Crarer, and Leroy D. Clark. *Employment Discrimination Law Cases.* 2d ed. Charlottesville, Va.: Bobbs-Merrill, 1982.

Sowell, Thomas. *Civil Rights: Rhetoric or Reality?* New York: Morrow, 1984.

Steiner, George. *Language and Silence: Essays on Language, Literature, and the Inhuman.* New York: Atheneum, 1967.

Taub, Nadine. "Keeping Women in Their Place: Stereotyping Per Se as a Form of Employment Discrimination." *Boston College Law Review* 21 (1980): 345–418.

Taylor, Ian, Paul Walton, and Jock Young. *The New Criminology: For a Social Theory of Deviance.* New York: Harper & Row, 1973.

TenBroek, Jacobus. *Equal under Law.* London: Collier, 1965.

Tocqueville, Alexis de. *Democracy in America.* Vol. 1. Edited by Francis Bowen. New York: Knopf, 1956.

Tormey, Judith Farr. "Exploitation, Oppression, and Self-Sacrifice." In *Women and Philosophy: Toward a Theory of Liberation*, edited by Carol C. Gould and Marx W. Wartofsky. New York: Putnam, 1976.

Tribe, Laurence H. "The Puzzling Persistence of Process-based Constitutional Theories." *Yale Law Journal* 89 (1980):1063–80.

Trubek, David M. "The Construction and Deconstruction of a Disputes-Focused Approach: An Afterword." *Law and Society Review* 15 (1980–81):727–47.

Trubek, David M., et al. *Civil Litigation Research Project: Final Report.* Law School, University of Wisconsin-Madison, 1983.

Tushnet, Mark. *The American Law of Slavery, 1810–1860: Considerations of Humanity and Interest.* Princeton: Princeton University Press, 1981.

Unger, Roberto. *The Critical Legal Studies Movement.* Cambridge: Harvard University Press, 1986.

Vining, Joseph. *Legal Identity: The Coming of Age of Public Man.* New Haven: Yale University Press, 1978.

Weber, Max. *Economy and Society.* Vol. 2. Edited by Guenther Roth and Claus Wittich. Berkeley and Los Angeles: University of California Press, 1968.

Wechsler, Herbert. "Toward Neutral Principles of Constitutional Law." *Harvard Law Review* 73 (1959): 1–35.

Weissberg, Liliane. "Writing on the Wall: Letters of Rahel Varnhagen." *New German Critique* 36 (1985):157–73.

West, Robin. "Authority, Autonomy, and Choice: The Role of Consent in the Moral and Political Visions of Franz Kafka and Richard Posner." *Harvard Law Review* 99 (1985):384–428.

Wilkinson, J. Harvie III. *From Brown to Bakke: The Supreme Court and School Integration, 1954–1978.* New York: Oxford University Press, 1979.

Wolfe, Alan. *The Limits of Legitimacy: Political Contradictions of Contemporary Capitalism.* New York: Free Press, 1978.

Wolfenstein, Eugene Victor. *The Victims of Democracy: Malcolm X and the Black Revolution.* Berkeley and Los Angeles: University of California Press, 1981.

Wolters, Raymond. *The Burden of Brown: Thirty Years of School Desegregation.* Knoxville: University of Tennessee Press, 1984.

Woodward, C. Vann. *The Strange Career of Jim Crow.* New York: Oxford University Press, 1955.

———. "Seeds of Failure in Radical Race Policy." In *New Frontiers of the American Reconstruction*, edited by Harold Hyman. Urbana: University of Illinois Press, 1966.

Young-Bruehl, Elisabeth. *Hannah Arendt: For the Love of the World.* New Haven: Yale University Press, 1982.

Zinn, Howard. "The Conspiracy of Law." In *The Rule of Law*, edited by Robert Paul Wolff, 15–36. New York: Simon & Schuster, 1971.

Index

Activism: during 1950s and 1960s, 46; focus on economic domination, 48; focus on voting rights, 95; and legal action, 51; rise and fall in, 1, 96; shift from religious to secular tone of, 47

Affirmative action: consequences of, 68; costs of, 13, 15; *Franks* case, 66; as violation of white employees' interests, 8

Age discrimination, 1, 53–55

Alienation: concept of, 62; surveys of, 114

American Dilemma, An (Myrdal), 5, 11, 50

Antidiscrimination doctrine, 1, 68, 102; actualized in social relations, 94; ideal and practice of, 25, 95; individualistic bias in, 16, 112; limitations of, 9, 10, 95; perpetrator's perspective in, 64–65; principle of neutrality in, 12; prototypical case, 9–10; reactivation of, 45; reference to standards, 9; separation of rights from remedy in, 21

Arendt, Hannah, 2; on Eichmann as villain, 77; on Rahel Varnhagen, 84–85; on respect, 97; on stigma, 17–18, 68

Assimilation: as goal of legal doctrine, 68; as response to discrimination, 84, 87–88

Authority: dependence on, 76; of legal rules, 110; paternalistic vision of, 78. *See also* Legal authority

Autobiography of Malcolm X, The, 86

Bell, Derrick, 20

Berger, Morroe, 4

Bettelheim, Bruno: extreme situations, 36, 74, 75; reintegration of victim's experiences, 77

Bilingual skills, 89

Black Codes, 42–43

Black Muslims, 86, 87

Black power, 19

Blacks, 5; as beneficiaries of the law, 44; and civil rights organizations, 46; historically disadvantaged, 117; as mothers, 14; as subjects of reform, 50

Black Skin, White Masks (Fanon), 63

Board of Regents of the University of California v. Bakke, 67, 115

Bona fide occupational qualifications, 8

Bradford v. Sloan Paper Co., 8

Brown v. Board of Education, 9, 11, 21, 67

Burden of proof, 7

Bus boycotts, 47, 48

Business necessity test, 8

Children: abused, 76; and school desegregation, 18, 68, 70

Children of Crisis (Coles), 70

Civil Litigation Research Project, 26, 27, 29

Civil rights: failure of strategies, 113; and ideal of equality, 4; modern view of, 45, 112; movement, 1, 6; proliferation of strategies, 51, 117; view of progress, 40

Civil Rights Act of 1964, 1, 8, 114; definition of discrimination in, 7; Title VII, 7, 8

Civil War: as constitutional revolution, 41; and democratic capitalism, 42

Coles, Robert, 70

Concentration camp prisoners, 36, 74, 75

Constitution, 65; original intent, 40; rhetorical evocation of, 46

Courts: appellate, 2, 64; as legal forum, 59; remedies from, 9, 37; state control of, 37

Criminal: defendants, 111; Joseph K. as, 106; Malcolm X as, 86; supervision of, 32; and victim relationship, 73

Criminal law: ideology of, 73; transformation of, 41, 51

Dahrendorf, Ralf, 35

Discrimination: acceptance of label, 52;

economics of, 15, 16; limitations on cases of, 7–8; link to economic inequality, 95; making claims of, 99–101; meaning of, 53; prevalence of, 101; sample of cases of, 26. *See also* Age discrimination; Race discrimination; Religious discrimination; Sex discrimination
Disparate impact, 8
Durkheim, Emile, 61

Economic models, 15–16; Becker-Arrow model, 15
Edelman, Murray, 65
Ellison, Ralph: on invisibility, 65; response to Arendt, 18
Ely, John Hart, 12
Emancipation Proclamation, 42
Employers: and affirmative action, 57; complaints to, 91, 93; discrimination by, 54, 90, 92; economic incentives of, 15–16; environment created by, 93–94; relationship of, with employees, 89; routine practices of, 99–100. *See also* Perpetrators of discrimination
Enticement laws, 44
Equal Employment Opportunity Commissions, 25, 105
Equal protection, 6, 13, 15, 67; suspect classification, 13, 61. *See also* Fourteenth Amendment
Exceptionality: avoidance of, 102; as device to show normality, 85–86
Exclusion: as response to discrimination, 84, 87–88; as strategy for empowerment, 86

Fanon, Frantz: guilt of oppressed, 72; heritage of domination, 67; image of masks, 63–64
Fate as female, 76
Feminist: disenchantment of groups, 109; label of, 101; view of legal reform, 21–22
Foucault, Michel, 2; ideological transformation, 41, 51; on individualization, 69; theory of social change, 113; view of legal power, 32–33; view of master-slave relation, 38
Fourteenth Amendment, 45; circumvention of, 43; commitment to principle

in, 40; historical intent, 6; and special protection, 61
Frank, Jerome, 24
Franks v. Bowman Transportation Co., 66
Freeman, Alan D., 20, 65
Fromm, Erich, 62
Fuller, Lon, 23

Genovese, Eugene: master–slave relationship, 72, 73, 74; rituals of slaves, 75
Glazer, Nathan, 14
Great Society, 96
Green v. County School Board, 11
Griffin, Susan, 75
Griggs v. Duke Power Co., 7, 21
Group: identity, 52, 71, 101; rights, 11, 13–14, 96–97
Guilt, of victims, 72, 105, 107

Harlan, John M., 65
Heller, Erich, 106
Hentig, Hans von, 73
Holocaust, definition of, 72

Ideology: definition of, 31; Foucault's view of, 33; historical creation of, 10; role in legal conflict, 4; study of, 34
Idolatry, 62–63
Individualism: and logic of equal protection, 14, 115–16; and meaning of rights, 102; neoconservative view of, 13
Injustice (Moore), 70
Intensive interviewing, 33–34
Invisibility: of blacks in the law, 44; sense of one's own, 99; of victims, 65–66
Invisible Man (Ellison), 65
Involuntary servitude. *See* Peonage

Janeway, Elizabeth, 76
Jesus as victim, 58–59
Jhering, Rodolph, 10
Judges, 12, 23, 32, 66

Kafka, Franz: *The Trial*, 106–7; image of legality, 116
King, Coretta Scott, 114
King, Martin Luther, 19, 47
Kirchheimer, Otto, 58

Law: corruption of, 104–5; as distinct from politics, 10; effectiveness of,

24–25; faith in, 4; fear of, 104–5; as instrument of power, 32, 37–38; language of, 30, 38; parable of, in *The Trial*, 106–7; thematization of, 36–37; views of, 98–99, 103. *See also* Private law

Lawyers, confidence game of, 34

Legal authority: images of, 30; as intruding presence, 60; realist critique of, 24

Legal conflict: alienation in, 62–63; balance of power within, 36–37, 108; evaluation of self-reports about, 30; rites of justice, 29; ritual form, 38; strategies in, 34–35

Legal consciousness: and mass consciousness, 31, 98; study of, 30, 34

Legal effectiveness: in antidiscrimination policies, 24–25; in Reconstruction policies, 44

Legal formalism, 23; in antidiscrimination law, 21

Legal identity: in judicial argument, 2, 60–61; multiple, 14; of slaves, 49

Legal protection, model of: and attitudes toward law, 98; critique of, 109–10, 116; definition of, 2; explanations for failure to make claims, 28–29; mobilization of law in, 10; and rational model, 25

Legal realism: critical strain of, 24; in law schools, 23

Legal reform: as defining purpose of law, 41; limitations on, 9, 114–15; through moral education, 5

Legal symbols: of hope, 20; of identity, 61

Liberal: dilemma, 5; disenchanted, 20; image of society, 19; view of discrimination, 114–15

Life chances, definition of, 35

Litigation: barriers to, 78, 98; versus grass-roots protest, 48–49; success of, 25, 28; propensity to, 27, 29; as rights-based strategy, 114; success of, 25, 28; as symbolic victory, 51

Little Rock incident, 17–18. *See also* School desegregation

Luhmann, Niklas, 36

Lukács, Georg, 31

Machiavelli, Niccolò, 80

Madison, James, and danger of

factions, 12

Malcolm X, 86–88

Mannheim, Karl, 30

Marcuse, Herbert: on art, 38; on guilt feelings of oppressed, 72; on ideology, 32

Marxist interpretation of law, 31

Masks: as alien, 63–64; in antidiscrimination doctrine, 64; false, 63; as metaphor in legal reasoning, 62

Mayhew, Leon, 25

Melting pot, view of society, 13

Miscegenation laws, 17

Moore, Barrington: on autonomy of oppressed, 70; on Civil War, 41

Moose Lodge v. Irvis, 6–7

Myrdal, Gunnar, 5, 11

National Association for the Advancement of Colored People (NAACP), 18; history and organization, 46

Nature of Prejudice, The (Allport), 82

Neoconservative view of discrimination: and belief in individual rights, 13; and competitive markets, 15; criticism of, 113, 114

Noonan, John, 62

Offe, Claus, 110

Parks, Rosa, 48

Passive protection, as Reconstruction strategy, 45

Peonage, 44

Perpetrators of discrimination: arbitrary power of, 78; and enforcement, 25–26; role in initiating conflict, 100–101; seen as enemies, 83; in state action doctrine, 6; tyrant image of, 3, 79–80. *See also* Employers

Persons and Masks of the Law (Noonan), 62

Plessy v. Ferguson, 43

Political trials, 58–59

Poor, 2, 76

Prejudice, theories of, 82–83

Prince, The (Machiavelli), 80

Prisons, failure of reform of, 32

Private law, 40, 44

Process theory, 11–13

Public versus private: and boundaries in

state action doctrine, 7; and economic interests of whites, 95; law, 40, 61; as social boundaries, 9, 17; and suppression of legal action, 29, 117

Race as social problem, 5
Race discrimination, 1, 56–58, 80, 88–89, 91–93; and ethnicity, 63, 89
Racism, 14, 19, 21, 46, 47, 115; prevalence of, 11
Radicals: criticism of, 113–14; view of discrimination, 19, 20–21
Rationality: and calculation of costs and benefits, 98; in exchange-like relations, 110; in extreme conditions, 74–75; and irrationality, 112
Rationalization: as data, 35–36; of modern law, 31
Reconstruction: expansion of judicial power, 43; reliance on legal procedures, 44; strategies, 3, 43
Religious discrimination, 17, 84–86
Representation of minorities, 12
Republic, The (Plato), 106
Rights: belief in, 5–6, 35; cost of invoking, 111; language of, 102, 112; myth of, 19–20; probability of enforcement, 35, 94; realized in person's lifetime, 94; radical critique of, 20–22; used as deterrent, 96; universalization of, 115–16, 117
Roles: conflicting, 103, 110; behavior, 64
Rose, Willie Lee, 49, 50
Rule of law, 110
Rules, skepticism about, 23–24. See also Law

Sacrifice: as endurance of mistreatment, 82–83; in historical context, 18; as martyrdom, 72; modern conditions of, 58; as personal decision, 94; for political ends, 58
Santayana, George, 64
Scheingold, Stuart, 20
School desegregation, 11, 70; and governmental purposes, 95; impact on majority, 65, Little Rock incident, 17–18, 68; path of reform in, 19–20
Segregation: employment, 16; social, 1, 9
Sennett, Richard: on authority, 94; on paternalism, 76

Sex discrimination, 1, 52–53, 55–56, 80, 81, 88, 90–91
Sexism, 11, 14, 19, 115
Sexual harassment: consequences of taking action against, 105; prevention of, 56; reaction to, 82, 90; as sex discrimination, 9; as strategy of legal protection, 51. See also Sex discrimination
Simmel, Georg, 71, 72
Slavery: and courts, 9; as domestic institution, 49, 50; growth as institution, 42; historical legacy of, 67; and moral guilt of reformers, 50; as moral issue, 42; reenactment of, 43; solutions to, 42
Slaves: identification with master, 50, 73; paternalistic ethos, 72; rituals, 75
Social psychology of victims, 3, 29, 76–77, 112–13
Socrates as victim, 58–59
Southern Christian Leadership Conference (SCLC): internal organizational struggle, 47; reaction to NAACP, 46; role in black activism, 46–48
Special protection: court rationale for, 5, 61; desirability of, 14; in a difference theory approach, 22. See also Equal protection
Split personality, of victims, 75
Standing, 60–61
State action doctrine, 6
Stigma, 67–68
Student Nonviolent Coordinating Committee (SNCC), 46
Supreme Court, U.S., 4, 6, 7, 8, 11, 12, 13, 20, 21, 42, 66, 67
Survival: and avoidance of reality, 74; honor as ethic of, 93; meaning of, 88; politics of, 70, 77; self-definition of, 3
Suspect classification. See Equal protection

Taney, Roger B., 42
Thirteenth Amendment, 45; commitment to principles in, 40; moral commitment of, 42
Title VII. See Civil Rights Act of 1964
Tocqueville, Alexis de, 2, 17; proclamation of rights, 102; shadow of the law, 60
Trial, The (Kafka), 106

Unemployment compensation, 55, 78

Varnhagen, Rahel, 84–86, 87–88
Victim: confusion of, 80–81; definition of, 58, 71; as evil, 74–75; in extreme conditions, 72; historical construction of, 49, 51, 66–67; and image of willing submissiveness, 73; label of, sanctions from, 27, 91, 103; legal role of, 52; multiple stress experienced by, 93; negative image of, 102; as political enemy, 65; self-respect of, 96–97; spirit and courage of, 69–70; view of the law, 2; violence and anger of, 57, 74, 81–82. *See also* Social psychology of victims; Victimhood; Victim-oppressor relationship
Victimhood: as collective phenomenon, 71; invisible bonds of, 3, 60, 74–77, 80–84, 111; as product of social imagination, 58
Victimology movement, 73
Victim-oppressor relationship, 3, 37, 71, 76–77, 80, 113; of criminals and victims, 73
Vietnam War protests, 47
Voting rights, 17; development of, 95

Weber, Max, 2
Witches, as victims and criminals, 74
Women: in economic ghettos, 16; images of, 53, 55–56, 68; orientation toward the law of, 22; separation of feeling from thought by, 75

The Civil Rights Society

Designed by Chris L. Smith
Composed by Rosedale Printing Company in Goudy Old Style with display lines in
    Futura Light
Printed by the Maple Press Company, Inc., on S. D. Warren's Sebago Eggshell Cream
    Offset paper and bound in Holliston's Payko #15380, with Multicolor endsheets in
    Presidential Blue and stamped in black